easy
summer food

easy summer food

simple recipes for sunny days

RYLAND
PETERS
& SMALL

LONDON NEW YORK

Designer Sarah Fraser

Commissioning Editor Elsa Petersen-Schepelern

Editor Sharon Cochrane

Production Gavin Bradshaw

Art Director Gabriella Le Grazie

Publishing Director Alison Starling

Index Hilary Bird

First published in the United States in 2005
by Ryland Peters & Small, Inc.
519 Broadway, 5th Floor
New York, NY 10012
www.rylandpeters.com

10 9 8 7 6 5 4 3

Text © Julz Beresford, Maxine Clark, Clare Ferguson,
Elsa Petersen-Schepelern, Louise Pickford, Fran Warde,
Lesley Waters, and Ryland Peters & Small 2005

Design and photographs © Ryland Peters & Small 2005

Library of Congress Cataloging-in-Publication Data

Easy summer food : simple recipes for sunny days.--
U.S. ed.
      p. cm.
Includes index.
ISBN 1-84172-824-1
1. Quick and easy cookery. 2. Summer.
TX833.5.E279 2005
641.5'64--dc22

                                           2004023987

Printed in China

Notes

All spoon measurements are level unless otherwise specified.

Ovens should be preheated to the specified temperature. If using a convection oven, cooking times should be reduced according to the manufacturer's instructions.

Uncooked or partially cooked eggs should not be served to the very young, the very old, those with compromised immune systems, or to pregnant women.

Speciality Asian ingredients are available in larger supermarkets and Asian stores.

To sterilize preserving jars, wash them in hot, soapy water and rinse in boiling water. Place in a large saucepan and then cover with hot water. With the saucepan lid on, bring the water to a boil and continue boiling for 15 minutes. Turn off the heat, then leave the jars in the hot water until just before they are to be filled. Sterilize the lids for 5 minutes, by boiling, or according to the manufacturer's instructions. Jars should be filled and sealed while they are still hot.

contents

a taste of summer   6

appetizers   8

salads   34

picnics   62

vegetables & vegetarian dishes   80

fish, meat, & poultry   92

pasta, pizza, & rice   114

grilling   138

dips & breads   174

sweet things & drinks   186

basics   224

index   236

credits   240

a taste of summer

Summer is about enjoying the outdoors and relaxing over good food with good company. Crisp salad greens, a handful of fresh berries, a scoop of ice cream, a cooling cocktail … these are the tastes of summer. This collection of recipes takes the best of the summer bounty and creates simple recipes to inspire you to make the most of what this fabulous season has to offer.

Covering everything from appetizers and entrées to sweet treats and cooling drinks, these easy recipes are all you need to enjoy summer to the full, whatever the occasion. Whether you are looking for a quick lunch for one, a stylish dinner for friends, or just something to cool and refresh, this book is packed with easy ideas. Eating outdoors is one of the pleasures of summer and with lots of recipes for picnics and grill parties, **Easy Summer Food** will encourage you to get out of the house and into the yard, the park, the beach, or wherever the sunshine happens to take you.

So, kick off your shoes, relax, and enjoy a delicious summer with this great selection of easy sunshine food.

appetizers

Gazpacho is a light summer soup. It originated in the south of Spain, traditionally in Andalusia. For best results use ripe tomatoes and a good-quality olive oil— but, most importantly, serve it icy cold.

gazpacho

Grind the garlic and a pinch of salt together using a mortar and pestle.

Put the bread in a saucer with a little water and let soak. Put the garlic, bread, tomatoes, onion, cucumber, and vinegar in a blender and purée until smooth. Keeping the machine running, add the oil in a slow and steady stream. Add salt and pepper to taste, then add the sugar.

Pour the mixture through a strainer into a bowl, adding more salt, pepper, and vinegar if necessary. Cover and chill in the refrigerator overnight. Serve it in small bowls or glasses with a little chopped cucumber sprinkled on top.

1 garlic clove

1 slice white bread, crusts removed

4 ripe juicy tomatoes, peeled and seeded

1 tablespoon grated onion

¼ small cucumber, peeled and seeded, plus extra to serve

1 tablespoon Spanish red wine vinegar

2 tablespoons olive oil

1 teaspoon sugar

sea salt and freshly ground black pepper

serves 4

On a hot summer's day, a chilled soup is the perfect appetizer or lunch dish. This coconut soup is based on an original Thai recipe—the contrast with the hot, aromatic garlic shrimp is just magical.

chilled coconut soup
with sizzling shrimp

2 cups coconut milk

1¼ cups plain yogurt

1 cucumber, peeled and chopped

2 tablespoons chopped fresh mint leaves

2 tablespoons extra virgin olive oil

2 garlic cloves, thinly sliced

½ teaspoon cumin seeds

a pinch of hot red pepper flakes

8–12 uncooked jumbo shrimp, peeled and deveined

sea salt and freshly ground black pepper

serves 4

Put the coconut milk, yogurt, cucumber, and mint in a blender or food processor and blend to a purée. Add salt and pepper to taste. Chill for 1 hour.

Ladle the soup into 4 bowls just before starting to cook the shrimp.

Put the oil in a large skillet and heat gently. Add the garlic, cumin seeds, and pepper flakes, and sauté very gently until the garlic is softened, but not golden. Using a slotted spoon, transfer the garlic mixture to a small plate.

Increase the heat under the skillet and add the shrimp. Stir-fry for 3 to 4 minutes until cooked through. Return the garlic mixture to the skillet, stir quickly, then immediately spoon the sizzling hot shrimp onto the soup and serve.

pappa al pomodoro

2 lb. ripe red tomatoes, preferably
on the vine, chopped

1¼ cups vegetable stock

1 teaspoon sugar

⅓ cup extra virgin olive oil

4 sprigs of oregano

4 sprigs of basil

4 slices dried bread,
without crusts

2 garlic cloves, cut in half

sea salt and freshly ground
black pepper

freshly grated Parmesan cheese,
to serve

serves 4

This is just one of those dishes that, once tasted, never forgotten. Pappa al pomodoro is a Tuscan "soup," although traditionally it is so thick you can almost eat it with a fork! This version is slightly more soup-like.

Put the tomatoes in a saucepan, add the stock, sugar, 2 tablespoons of the oil, and the leaves from the oregano and most of the basil leaves, reserving a few for serving. Add a little salt and pepper, then heat slowly to boiling point. Reduce the heat, cover, and simmer gently for 30 minutes.

Toast the bread over a preheated medium-hot outdoor grill or on a stove-top grill pan until barred with brown. Rub the bread all over with the garlic, then transfer to a plate. Sprinkle with the remaining oil and, using a fork, mash well into the bread, breaking it into small bits.

Add the bread to the soup and stir over low heat for about 5 minutes until the bread has been evenly incorporated and the soup has thickened.

Add salt and pepper to taste and serve hot, topped with a little grated Parmesan and the reserved basil leaves. This dish is also delicious served cold.

Put the bagna cauda–the "hot bath"–of warm anchovy butter in the center of the table with a basket of fresh summer vegetables, so everyone can just help themselves.

summer vegetables
with bagna cauda

8 oz. fresh, young, summer vegetables for each serving, such as baby carrots, baby fennel bulbs, radishes, cherry tomatoes, and baby zucchini, washed and trimmed

bagna cauda

4 tablespoons unsalted butter

3–4 large garlic cloves, crushed

2 oz. canned anchovies in oil, drained and chopped

¾ cup extra virgin olive oil

serves 4–6

Arrange the trimmed vegetables in a basket or on a large platter.

To make the bagna cauda, put the butter and garlic in a small saucepan and heat gently. Simmer very slowly for 4 to 5 minutes until the garlic has softened, but not browned. Add the anchovies, stir well, then pour in the oil. Cook gently for a further 10 minutes, stirring occasionally, until the sauce is soft and almost creamy.

Transfer the sauce to a dish and serve at once with the selection of trimmed vegetables.

All the colors of the Italian flag are here—red, white, and green. This makes a great start to a rustic summer meal. Bocconcini (meaning "little bites") are tiny balls of mozzarella. They are the perfect size for bruschetta but, if you can't find them, use regular mozzarella instead and cut it into cubes.

cherry tomato, bocconcini, and basil bruschetta

Put 3 tablespoons of the olive oil and the balsamic vinegar in a bowl and beat. Season to taste with salt and pepper. Stir in the halved bocconcini or mozzarella cubes, tomatoes, and torn basil leaves.

To make the bruschetta, grill, toast, or pan-grill the bread on both sides until lightly browned or toasted. Rub the top side of each slice with the cut garlic, then sprinkle with ½ tablespoon olive oil.

Cover each slice of bruschetta with arugula and spoon the tomatoes and mozzarella on top. Sprinkle with the remaining olive oil and top with fresh basil leaves.

4½ tablespoons extra virgin olive oil

1 teaspoon balsamic vinegar

12 bocconcini cheeses, cut in half, or 13 oz. regular mozzarella cheese, cubed

20 ripe cherry tomatoes or pomodorini (baby plum tomatoes), cut in half

a handful of torn fresh basil leaves, plus extra to serve

4 thick slices rustic bread, preferably sourdough

2 garlic cloves, cut in half

1 cup arugula

sea salt and freshly ground black pepper

serves 4

Radicchio, the bitter red Italian endive, is used as a salad leaf and also cooked as a vegetable. The round-headed Verona variety is available all year round, while Treviso, the version with long leaves, is usually available only during fall and winter. If you can't find them, use another bitter green, such as frisée or escarole, instead. Teamed with velvety blue Gorgonzola cheese and walnuts, this is an utterly irresistible combination.

radicchio with gorgonzola and walnuts

4–5 oz. Gorgonzola cheese

1 head of radicchio

1 head of Treviso or other bitter green

2 tablespoons extra virgin olive oil (optional)

¾ cup shelled walnuts or pecans

freshly ground black pepper

serves 4

Slice or break the cheese into 2-inch wedges or chunks.

Separate the radicchio and Treviso into leaves.

Arrange the leaves on small serving plates and drizzle with olive oil, if using. Add the Gorgonzola and walnuts or pecans, then serve, sprinkled with freshly ground black pepper.

Asparagus in season is pure delight and, whether it is the fine wild variety or the large cultivated type, it is considered a particular treat in Europe. Add the delicate sweetness of prosciutto, dried to crispness, and you have an unusual combination. Use white asparagus if you can find it (French and Italian grocers often stock this during early summer), although green asparagus is more usual.

asparagus with prosciutto

8 thin slices prosciutto, such as Parma ham, San Danièle, or jamón serrano, 6–7 oz.

1 lb. bunch of thick asparagus

2 tablespoons extra virgin olive oil or lemon-infused olive oil

a shallow baking tray

serves 4

Before turning on the oven, hang the slices of prosciutto over the grids of the top oven rack. Slide the rack into the oven, then turn it on to 300°F. Leave for 20 minutes or until the prosciutto has dried and become crisp. Remove it carefully and set aside.

Using a vegetable peeler, peel 3 inches of the tough skin off the end of each asparagus spear, then snap off and discard any tough ends. Arrange the asparagus on a shallow baking tray and sprinkle with the oil. Cook under a preheated broiler for 6 to 8 minutes, or until the asparagus is wrinkled and tender.

Serve the asparagus with some of the hot oil from the broiler pan and 2 prosciutto "crisps" for each person.

marinated anchovies

People tend to be intimidated by these little fish,
but have no fear, they are easy to prepare and taste
simply divine. Soon, you will be using these little
gems with everything.

6 oz. fresh anchovies*

*scant ½ cup good-quality
white vinegar*

3 garlic cloves, sliced

*1 tablespoon chopped fresh
flat-leaf parsley*

scant ½ cup olive oil

serves 4

**If fresh anchovies are
unavailable, use any small
fish, such as smelts or
tiny sardines. Aim for
2–3 inches long.*

To clean the anchovies, run your finger down the belly side and open up the fish. Pull the spine from the head and separate it from the flesh. Remove the head. Wash the fish and pat dry on paper towels.

Put the anchovies in a plastic container and pour in the vinegar. Let marinate in the refrigerator overnight. Rinse the anchovies and put in a serving dish with the garlic, parsley, and oil, cover, and chill overnight in the refrigerator. Return to room temperature before serving with bread or as an accompaniment to another dish. You can return them to the refrigerator to eat another day—they only get better with time.

A mousseline is a mousse of fish, shellfish, or poultry lightened with cream and egg whites. When made with salmon, it is the most beautiful, elegant, golden-pink. It is amazingly easy to prepare too, with a spectacular effect that makes a luxurious appetizer or posh picnic dish.

smoked and fresh salmon terrine

8 oz. skinless salmon fillet, cut into chunks

1 teaspoon finely grated unwaxed orange zest

2 teaspoons freshly squeezed orange juice

¼ cup chopped fresh dill or chervil

14 oz. smoked salmon

2 egg whites, chilled

⅔ cup heavy cream, chilled

freshly ground white pepper

red salad leaves, to serve

4-cup terrine mold, lightly oiled and base-lined with wax paper

serves 6

Put the chunks of fresh salmon in a food processor with the orange zest, orange juice, dill or chervil, and plenty of pepper. Blend until smooth. Remove the bowl from the food processor, cover, and chill in the refrigerator.

Meanwhile, coarsely chop half the smoked salmon. Put the bowl back on the processor. With the machine running, add the egg whites through the feed tube, then the cream. Blend until thick and smooth—do not overwork or it will curdle. Scrape into a bowl and stir in the chopped smoked salmon. Carefully fill the prepared mold with the mixture, packing down well. Level the surface and cover the top with buttered wax paper. Stand the terrine in a roasting pan and pour in hot water to come halfway up the sides. Bake in a preheated oven at 350°F for 35 to 40 minutes until firm.

Remove from the oven, let cool completely, then chill in the refrigerator. Loosen the edges with a thin knife and turn out onto a wooden board. Trim and tidy up the edges and pat dry. Wrap the terrine with the remaining smoked salmon, pressing down well, then transfer to a flat serving platter. Slice the terrine with a very sharp knife and serve with red salad leaves.

This classic tapas dish is served just about everywhere in Spain. The way to make sure this dish is tender is to buy small squid and not cook them too long.

fried squid roman-style

1 lb. small squid, or 6 oz. cleaned squid tubes

2 eggs

all-purpose flour, for dusting

olive oil, for frying

sea salt

1 lemon, cut into wedges, to serve

an electric deep-fryer

serves 4

To clean the squid, pull the head away from the body (tube). Rub your thumb down the length of the tube and lever off the wings and discard. Remove the translucent quill inside and rub the pink skin off the outside. Wash well under cold water. Cut the tubes into ½-inch slices.

Put the eggs in a bowl, add 2 tablespoons water, and beat well. Put the flour on a plate and sprinkle generously with salt. Working on one squid ring at a time, dip them into the egg mixture, then into the flour, making sure they are well coated. Set aside.

Fill a deep-fryer with oil to the manufacturer's recommended level and heat to 380°F. Working in batches, cook the squid rings until golden brown. (Make sure that the temperature remains the same for each batch.) Remove with a slotted spoon and drain on crumpled paper towels. Let rest for 5 minutes, then serve with the lemon wedges.

Yogurt-crusted chicken threaded onto skewers makes ideal finger food for an informal start to a meal. The yogurt tenderizes the chicken and helps the lemon soak into the meat. For the best flavor, cook them on an outdoor grill—the yogurt becomes delicious and slightly crunchy.

chicken and lemon skewers

Cut the chicken lengthwise into ⅛-inch strips and put in a shallow ceramic dish.

Put all the marinade ingredients in a bowl, stir well, and pour over the chicken. Turn to coat, cover, and let marinate in the refrigerator overnight.

The next day, thread the chicken onto the soaked bamboo skewers, zig-zagging the meat back and forth as you go.

Cook on a preheated outdoor grill or under a hot broiler for 3 to 4 minutes on each side until lightly charred and tender. Let cool slightly before serving.

1 lb. skinless, boneless chicken breast portions

marinade

1 cup plain yogurt

2 tablespoons extra virgin olive oil

2 garlic cloves, crushed

grated zest and freshly squeezed juice of 1 unwaxed lemon

1–2 teaspoons ground chiles

1 tablespoon chopped fresh cilantro

sea salt and freshly ground black pepper

12 bamboo skewers, soaked in cold water for 30 minutes

serves 4

This tapas dish is simple and delicious. Chorizo comes in many different varieties—smoked, unsmoked, fresh, and cured. Here, try using spicy fresh chorizo, available in Mexican markets. Large quantities of paprika give a rich color and pungent flavor.

chorizo in red wine

1 tablespoon olive oil

10 oz. small, spicy fresh chorizo sausages, cut into ½-inch slices

½ cup red wine

crusty bread, to serve

serves 4

Put the oil in a heavy skillet and heat until smoking. Add the chorizo and cook for 1 minute. Reduce the heat, add the wine, and cook for 5 minutes.

Transfer to a serving dish and set aside to develop the flavors. Serve warm with crusty bread.

salads

The famous Italian caprese salad normally includes basil. In this variation, arugula adds an intriguing, peppery bite. Do use milky, soft *mozzarella di bufala*, made from the rich, very white milk of water buffaloes, not cows. Add red-ripe, flavorful tomatoes and a good-quality extra virgin olive oil and this dish becomes sublime.

mozzarella, tomato, and arugula salad

Drain the mozzarellas. Slice thickly or pull them apart into big rough chunks, showing the grainy strands. Arrange down one side of a large serving platter.

Slice the tomatoes thickly and arrange them in a second line down the middle of the plate. If they are very large, cut them in half first, then into semicircles. Add the wild arugula leaves down the other side of the platter.

Sprinkle with salt and pepper, then just before serving trickle the olive oil over the top. Make sure you have crusty bread (slightly char-grilled tastes good) to mop up the juices.

variation Sharp, herbed black olives may also be added.

3 buffalo mozzarella cheeses, 5 oz. each

4 large, juicy, sun-ripened red tomatoes

4 large handfuls of arugula, about 3 cups

about ½ cup extra virgin olive oil, preferably Italian

sea salt and freshly ground black pepper

crusty bread, to serve

serves 4

caesar salad

This is probably the most famous salad in the world and the perfect combination of salty, crispy crunch. It seems to have been around forever, but not so—it was invented by Italian chef Caesar Cardini in Tijuana, Mexico, in 1924. Note that this recipe serves one person—just multiply the ingredients to serve more people.

1 egg, preferably farm-fresh and organic

6 smallest leaves of romaine lettuce

½ tablespoon freshly squeezed lemon juice

2 tablespoons extra virgin olive oil

3–4 canned anchovy fillets, rinsed and drained

Parmesan cheese, at room temperature, shaved into curls with a vegetable peeler

sea salt and freshly ground black pepper

1 lemon cut into wedges, to serve (optional)

croutons

1 thick slice crusty white bread or challah bread

1 garlic clove, crushed

2 tablespoons oil or softened butter

serves 1

To cook the egg, put it in a small saucepan of water and bring to a boil. Reduce the heat and simmer for 4 to 5 minutes. Remove from the heat and cover with cold water to stop it cooking further. Let cool a little, then peel. Cut into fourths just before serving.

To make the croutons, tear the bread into bite-size chunks*, rub with the garlic, and brush with oil or butter. Cook on a preheated stove-top grill pan until crisply golden and barred with brown.

Put the lettuce in a large bowl and sprinkle with salt and pepper, add the lemon juice, and toss with your hands. Sprinkle with olive oil and toss again.

Put the croutons in a bowl and put the dressed greens on top. Add the anchovies, egg, and Parmesan, sprinkle with pepper, and serve with lemon wedges, if using.

*note The croutons were traditionally made of sliced bread cut into cubes. Here they are made freeform, so you get lots of crisp, crunchy edges. Be classic if you prefer.

Avocado is so creamy and delicious it can be used as a dressing in itself. You can mix avocado with whatever looks good that day—shrimp, crab, smoked fish, or smoked chicken—top it just with a few herb leaves, lots of pepper, a squeeze of lemon juice, and eat it without any dressing. If you have to share it with others, by all means serve it with these salad greens and a regular dressing.

avocado salad

6 very thin slices prosciutto or bacon

1 tablespoon olive oil

8 oz. salad greens—a mixture of soft, crisp, and peppery

1–2 ripe Hass avocados*, cut in half and pits removed

dressing

⅓ cup extra virgin olive oil

1 tablespoon cider vinegar or rice vinegar

1 garlic clove, crushed

1 teaspoon Dijon mustard

sea salt and freshly ground black pepper

serves 4

If using prosciutto, cut the slices into 3 to 4 pieces. Heat a skillet, brush with 1 tablespoon olive oil, add the prosciutto or bacon, and cook at medium heat, without disturbing the pieces, until crisp on one side. Using tongs, turn the slices over and sauté until crisp and papery but not too brown. Remove and drain on paper towels.

To make the dressing, put the oil, vinegar, garlic, mustard, salt, and pepper in a salad bowl and beat with a fork or small whisk. When ready to serve, add the greens and turn in the dressing, using your hands. Using a teaspoon, scoop out balls of avocado into the salad. Toss gently if you like (although this will send the avocado to the bottom of the bowl). Add the crisp prosciutto or bacon and serve immediately.

*note To test an avocado for ripeness, don't stick your thumb in it. Cradle it in the palm of your hand and squeeze gently. If it just gives to the pressure, it's perfect.

Greek salads are so much part of the easy, Mediterranean style of eating—a bit of crisp, a bit of fiery, a few baby herbs, some vinegary olives (and Greece produces some of the best), and salty anchovies. Unpitted Kalamata olives are used in this recipe because they have more flavor—warn your guests in case they're not expecting them.

big greek salad

1 head iceberg lettuce, cut into fourths and torn apart

about 8 oz. feta cheese, crumbled into big pieces, or cut into cubes

1½ cups Kalamata olives

2 red onions, cut in half, then sliced into petals

2 Kirby cucumbers, cut in half lengthwise, then thinly sliced diagonally

4 big ripe red tomatoes, cut into chunks

8 anchovies*, or to taste

a few sprigs of oregano, torn

a few sprigs of mint, torn

greek dressing

⅓ cup extra virgin olive oil, preferably Greek

2 tablespoons freshly squeezed lemon juice

sea salt and freshly ground black pepper

serves 4

Put the lettuce in a large bowl. Add the feta, olives, onions, cucumbers, and tomatoes.

To make the dressing, put the olive oil, lemon juice, salt, and pepper in a bowl, beat with a fork, then pour over the salad. You can also sprinkle them onto the salad separately.

Top with the anchovies, oregano, and mint, and serve.

*note Greek markets sell salted anchovies in big cans—wheels of whole fish, arranged nose to tail. You rinse and fillet them yourself. However, if you don't have a Greek market, use canned ones instead. Rinse and drain them before adding them to the salad.

A beautiful, delicious, simple salad based on the classic *Insalata Caprese*. If you can't find the most important ingredient for the original salad (the very best, ripest, most flavorful tomatoes), bell peppers are a great solution.

italian broiled bell pepper salad

4 large red bell peppers or Cubanelle

2 mozzarella cheeses, preferably buffalo mozzarella, about 8 oz.

4 handfuls of arugula, torn

¼ cup best-quality, extra virgin olive oil

balsamic vinegar (optional)

sea salt and freshly ground black pepper

serves 4

Put the whole bell peppers under a hot broiler, on a grill, or over the flame of a gas stove. Cook on all sides until charred. Remove from the heat, transfer to a saucepan, and put on the lid (this will help steam off the skins).

When cool, drain the juices into a small bowl. Scrape off and discard the charred skins. Cut the peppers in half lengthwise and scrape out and discard the seeds and membranes, adding any juices to the bowl.

To make the dressing, put 2 tablespoons of the pepper juices in another bowl with the olive oil and beat with a fork. Add salt and pepper to taste, and extra pepper juice if you like. (Keep any extra juice for another use.)

When ready to assemble the salad, tear the mozzarellas into big shreds—about 4 pieces each—and divide between 4 chilled plates. Add a handful of arugula and 2 bell pepper halves to each plate. Sprinkle with the olive oil, then add a few drops of balsamic*, if using, to each serving. Sprinkle with sea salt flakes and pepper and serve.

*note Don't slather the balsamic over the salad. Use it as a seasoning, not a dressing.

6 very ripe tomatoes

2 garlic cloves, thinly sliced

4 thick slices day-old bread, preferably Italian-style, such as pugliese or ciabatta

about 4 inches cucumber, cut in half, seeded, and thinly sliced diagonally

1 red onion, chopped

1 tablespoon chopped fresh flat-leaf parsley

½–¾ cup extra virgin olive oil

2 tablespoons white wine vinegar, cider vinegar, or sherry vinegar

a bunch of basil, leaves torn

12 caperberries or ¼ cup capers packed in brine, rinsed and drained

1 teaspoon balsamic vinegar (optional)

sea salt and freshly ground black pepper

serves 4

There are as many variations of this Tuscan bread salad as there are cooks. The trick is to let the flavors blend well without the bread becoming mushy. Always use the ripest, reddest, most flavorful tomatoes you can find, like Brandywine, or one of the other full-flavored heirloom varieties, such as Black Russian or Green Zebra, or at least an Italian plum tomato.

tuscan panzanella

Cut the tomatoes in half, spike with slivers of garlic, and roast in a preheated oven at 350°F for about 1 hour, or until wilted and some of the moisture has evaporated.

Meanwhile, put the bread on an oiled stove-top grill pan and cook on both sides, until lightly toasted and barred with grill marks. Tear or cut the toast into pieces and put in a salad bowl. Sprinkle with a little water until damp.

Add the tomatoes, cucumber, onion, parsley, salt, and pepper. Sprinkle with the olive oil and vinegar, toss well, then set aside for about 1 hour to develop the flavors.

Add the basil leaves, caperberries or capers, and sprinkle with a few drops of balsamic vinegar, if using, then serve.

quick chickpea salad

2 cups cooked or canned
chickpeas, rinsed and drained
(2 cans, 15 oz. each)

4 marinated artichoke hearts

4 large semi-dried tomatoes
(optional)*

8 oz. very ripe cherry tomatoes,
cut in half

8 scallions, sliced diagonally

a handful of fresh basil
leaves, torn

a small bunch of fresh chives,
snipped

leaves from 4 sprigs of flat-leaf
parsley, chopped

2 oz. fresh Parmesan
cheese, shaved

1 tablespoon black pepper,
cracked with a mortar and pestle

dijon dressing

⅓ cup extra virgin olive oil

1 tablespoon freshly squeezed
lemon juice or sherry vinegar

1 teaspoon Dijon mustard

1 small garlic clove, crushed

sea salt and freshly ground
black pepper

serves 4

Chickpeas are a great ingredient for lunchtime salads and as a vegetable entrée accompaniment. Like all dried legumes, they drink up flavors, but unlike some, chickpeas can be relied upon not to fall apart. They're perfect for picnics and other make-ahead occasions. You can part-prepare them, so the dressing soaks into the chickpeas, then add the fresh ingredients just before serving.

Put the dressing ingredients in a bowl and beat with a fork. Add the chickpeas, artichoke hearts, and semi-dried tomatoes, if using, and toss in the dressing. Cover and chill for up to 4 hours.

When ready to serve, add the cherry tomatoes, scallions, basil, chives, and parsley. Stir gently, sprinkle with the shaved Parmesan and pepper, then serve.

*note Use partially sun-dried tomatoes, sometimes called sun-blushed, which are sold in Italian gourmet stores.

variations You can add any number of other ingredients, including olives, prosciutto, salami, or sautéed chorizo, canned or fresh tuna, other vegetables, lettuces or herbs, or your favorite spices.

A few drops of chile oil in the dressing instead of the mustard give a different kind of fire.

Tabbouleh, the fresh parsley salad from Lebanon, is based on bulgur wheat. This version is made with couscous, the fine Moroccan pasta, now available in an instant version—you just soak it in water or stock for 10 minutes or so.

fragrant herb couscous salad

1½ cups couscous

freshly squeezed juice of 1 lemon

2 tablespoons chopped fresh basil leaves

2 tablespoons chopped fresh cilantro

2 tablespoons chopped fresh mint leaves

2 tablespoons chopped fresh parsley

sea salt and freshly ground black pepper

2 lemons, cut in half, to serve (optional)

fragrant garlic oil

1 whole head of garlic, cloves separated

2 bay leaves

2¾ cups extra virgin olive oil

serves 4

To make the fragrant oil, peel the garlic cloves and put them in a saucepan. Add the bay leaves and oil and heat gently for 15 minutes until the garlic has softened. Don't let the garlic brown. Let cool, remove and mash the garlic cloves, then return them to the oil. Chill until required. Use 1¼ cups for this recipe and reserve the remainder.

Put the couscous in a bowl, add water to cover by 2 inches, and let soak for 10 minutes.

Drain the soaked couscous, shaking the strainer well to remove any excess water. Transfer to a bowl, add the fragrant garlic oil, lemon juice, chopped basil, cilantro, mint, and parsley. Season with salt and pepper, then set aside to develop the flavors until ready to serve. Serve with halved lemons, if using.

New Zealanders go wild for their tiny, white, marble-size new potatoes. They are mostly consumed locally, but a small surplus is exported to Australia and California. When you have grown bored with eating them plain, or with butter or olive oil and herbs, there are some other interesting dressings to explore. This one includes canned smoked oysters, fresh lime juice, and superb extra virgin olive oil—although it looks messy and odd, it tastes gorgeous.

antipodean potato salad

5 cups marble-size new potatoes, about 1½ lb., scrubbed

⅔ cup extra virgin olive oil

½ cup canned smoked oysters, drained

2 teaspoons Dijon mustard

freshly squeezed juice of 1 lime

2 garlic cloves, crushed

2–3 teaspoons mild paprika

sea salt flakes and freshly ground black pepper

a bunch of fresh chives, snipped, or a few sprigs of basil, to serve

serves 6

Cook the potatoes in boiling salted water for 15 to 18 minutes, or until tender. Drain. Crush them very gently and lightly with a fork, then return them to the still-hot pan. Drizzle with about half the olive oil, then sprinkle with salt and pepper.

To make the dressing, put the remaining oil, smoked oysters, mustard, lime juice, garlic, and paprika in a blender and process to form a creamy emulsion. Trickle half the dressing over the warm potatoes and serve the rest separately. Sprinkle with chives or basil, then serve warm or cool.

variation For a sensational shocking pink salad dressing, omit the smoked oysters and use another famous New Zealand product, the tamarillo, instead. Cut 2 ripe tamarillos in half and scoop out the red flesh. Blend with the other dressing ingredients for a vivid, colorful vegetarian dressing.

salade niçoise

A classic composed salad from the south of France, salade Niçoise makes a wonderful lunch for four or an appetizer for eight.

10–12 small salad potatoes, such as fingerlings

olive oil, for tossing the potatoes

4 eggs

1 cup shelled fava beans or baby lima beans, fresh or frozen, or 6 cooked baby artichokes, cut in half

4 oz. green beans, trimmed

3 scallions, cut in half lengthwise

2 small red onions, cut in half lengthwise

2 Kirby cucumbers or 8 inches regular cucumber, unwaxed

2 red or yellow bell peppers, peeled (see method)

4 romaine heart leaves or other crisp lettuce leaves

1 basket cherry tomatoes, about 20, cut in half

1 small can anchovies, drained

1 large can or jar good-quality tuna packed in olive oil, drained

about 20 Niçoise black olives

about 20 caperberries or 3 tablespoons salt-packed capers, rinsed and drained

a large handful of fresh basil leaves

vinaigrette

⅓ cup extra virgin olive oil

1 tablespoon white wine vinegar, cider vinegar, or sherry vinegar

1 teaspoon Dijon mustard (optional)

1 garlic clove, crushed

sea salt and freshly ground black pepper

serves 8 as a appetizer, 4 as an entrée

Cook the potatoes in boiling salted water until tender, about 10 minutes. Drain and plunge them into a bowl of ice water with ice cubes. Let cool. Drain, then toss in a little olive oil and cut in half.

Put the eggs in a saucepan of cold water, bring to a boil, reduce the heat, and simmer for 5 minutes. Drain, then cover with cold water. When cool, peel, then cut in half just before serving.

Steam the fava beans or lima beans, if using, and green beans separately until tender. Plunge into ice water, then pop each fava bean out of its skin. Blanch the scallions for 30 seconds in boiling water. Drain and plunge into ice water. Alternatively, leave uncooked.

Thinly slice the red onions and cucumbers, preferably on a mandoline—slice the cucumbers diagonally. If peeling the bell peppers, do so using a vegetable peeler, then cut off the top and bottom, open out, seed, and cut the flesh into thick strips.

Put the lettuce leaves on a platter. Add bundles of green beans and scallions, then the potatoes, fava or lima beans or artichokes, halved eggs, tomatoes, cucumber, onions, and bell peppers. Top with anchovy fillets or tuna, black olives, caperberries or capers, and basil leaves.

To make the vinaigrette, mix all the ingredients in a small pitcher and serve separately.

Tonno e fagioli–tuna and beans. This simple Italian dish is great when you come home from work, all the stores have shut, and you've run out of almost everything. Although any dolphin-friendly canned tuna is fine, it will be fabulously good if you use top-quality French or Italian tuna. Cannellini beans can be delicate, so toss them gently. Though not traditional, you could make this with chickpeas, lentils, or pinto beans, instead of the cannellini beans.

tonno e fagioli

1–2 large garlic cloves, crushed

1 tablespoon sherry vinegar or white wine vinegar

⅓ cup extra virgin olive oil

4 cups cooked or canned cannellini or other white beans (2 cans, 15 oz. each) rinsed and drained

2 red onions, thinly sliced into petals, then blanched,* or 6 small scallions, sliced

14 oz. can or jar best-quality tuna

a few handfuls of fresh basil leaves

sea salt and freshly ground black pepper

serves 6

Put the garlic on a cutting board, crush with the flat of a knife, add a large pinch of salt, then mash to a paste with the tip of the knife. Transfer to a bowl, add the vinegar and 2 tablespoons of the oil, and beat with a fork.

Add the beans and onions and toss gently. Taste, then add extra olive oil and vinegar to taste.

Drain the tuna and separate into large chunks. Add to the bowl and turn gently to coat with the dressing. Top with the basil and black pepper.

*note Blanching is optional, but it takes the edge off the sharpness of the onions. To blanch them, put them in a saucepan of boiling water, boil for 1 minute, then remove from the heat, and drain well.

With its rich, almost plum-like flavors of raisins and Marsala, this salad is a real treat. Sherry vinegar is sold in larger supermarkets or gourmet stores. If you can't find it, use balsamic instead.

chicken salad
with radicchio and pine nuts

Put the onion slices in a small bowl and cover with cold water. Let soak for 30 minutes, drain well, then pat dry with paper towels.

Tear or slice the chicken into thin strips and put in a large salad bowl. Add the radicchio, arugula (leaves torn if large), parsley, and onion.

To make the dressing, put 2 tablespoons of the oil in a skillet, heat gently, add the pine nuts and raisins, and sauté for 3 to 4 minutes until the pine nuts are lightly golden. Add the Marsala and vinegar, with salt and pepper to taste, and warm through. Stir in the remaining oil and remove from the heat.

Pour the dressing over the salad, toss lightly, and serve.

1 small red onion, sliced

1½ lb. cooked chicken breast

1 head of radicchio, shredded

1 cup arugula

a few sprigs of flat-leaf parsley

marsala raisin dressing

⅓ cup extra virgin olive oil

½ cup pine nuts

½ cup raisins

2 tablespoons Marsala wine

2 tablespoons sherry vinegar

sea salt and freshly ground black pepper

serves 4–6

One great thing about many Thai dishes is their use of fresh herbs. They are often flooded with the pungent flavors of Thai basil, mint, and cilantro. Thai basil is available from Asian stores, but you could use regular basil instead. Bok choy is also known as "pak choi."

thai-style beef salad

1 tablespoon Szechuan peppercorns, or black peppercorns, lightly crushed

1 teaspoon ground coriander

1 teaspoon sea salt

1 lb. beef tenderloin, in one piece

1 tablespoon peanut or canola oil

1 cucumber, thinly sliced

4 scallions, thinly sliced

2 baby bok choy, thinly sliced

a handful of fresh Thai basil leaves

a handful of fresh mint leaves

a handful of fresh cilantro

lime dressing

1 tablespoon palm sugar or brown sugar

1 tablespoon Thai fish sauce

2 tablespoons freshly squeezed lime juice

2 small, hot red chile peppers, such as bird's eye, seeded and chopped

1 garlic clove, crushed

serves 4

Put the peppercorns, coriander, and salt onto a plate and mix. Rub the beef all over with the oil, then put onto the plate and turn to coat with the spices.

Cook the beef on a preheated outdoor grill or stove-top grill pan for about 10 minutes, turning to brown evenly. Remove from the heat and let cool.

Meanwhile, to make the dressing, put the sugar in a saucepan, add the fish sauce and 2 tablespoons water, and heat until the sugar dissolves. Remove the pan from the heat, let cool, then stir in the lime juice, chiles, and garlic.

Cut the beef into thin slices and put in a large bowl. Add the cucumber, scallions, bok choy, and herbs. Pour the dressing over the top, toss well, and serve.

picnics

Black olives, which have already been cured, will mellow even more if you crack them a little or prick with a fork, then marinate in aromatics and fine olive oil as they do in Morocco. Experiment until you find a flavor you like—your own customized blend. If you were to use Moroccan oil in this recipe, the result would be really authentic, but any robust extra virgin will do.

marinated black olives

3 cups black olives in brine

2 tablespoons fennel or cumin seeds, crushed

1 tablespoon green cardamom pods, crushed

1 tablespoon small hot dried red chiles

2 tablespoons allspice berries, crushed

3–4 cups extra virgin olive oil

12 fresh bay leaves, washed, dried, and bruised

8-inch strip of orange zest, bruised

1 large jar (6 cups) or 3 jars (2 cups each), sterilized

makes 6–7 cups

Rinse the olives in cold water, drain, then pat dry with paper towels.

Put them on a clean, dry surface such as a cutting board and crush them slightly with a meat bat or rolling pin, or prick with a fork, to open up the flesh a little.

Put the fennel or cumin, cardamom, chiles, and allspice in a dry skillet and toast over moderate heat for a few minutes until aromatic.

Put the olive oil in a saucepan and heat to 350°F—a cube of bread should turn golden-brown in 40 to 50 seconds. Let cool a little. Using a sterilized spoon, pack the zest, bay leaves, olives, and spices into the jar, or jars, in layers, until they all have been used. Cover with the hot oil. Let cool, uncovered. When cold, seal and store in a cool, dark place.

Leave for at least 1 week before tasting. These olives keep well and improve for some months.

With its lovely, earthy flavors, a frittata is an Italian version of the Spanish tortilla or the French omelet and different ingredients are added depending on the region or season.

mixed mushroom frittata

3 tablespoons extra virgin olive oil

2 shallots, finely chopped

2 garlic cloves, finely chopped

1 tablespoon chopped fresh thyme leaves

3 cups mixed wild and cultivated mushrooms, such as chanterelle, portobello, shiitake, and white mushrooms

6 eggs

2 tablespoons chopped fresh flat-leaf parsley

sea salt and freshly ground black pepper

serves 6

Put 2 tablespoons of the oil into a nonstick skillet, heat gently, then add the shallots, garlic, and thyme. Sauté gently for 5 minutes until softened but not browned.

Meanwhile, brush off any dirt clinging to the mushrooms and wipe the caps. Chop or slice coarsely and add to the skillet. Sauté for 4 to 5 minutes until they are just starting to release their juices. Remove from the heat.

Put the eggs in a bowl with the parsley and a little salt and pepper, beat briefly, then stir in the mushroom mixture. Wipe the skillet clean.

Heat the remaining tablespoon of oil in the clean skillet and pour in the egg and mushroom mixture. Cook over medium heat for 8 to 10 minutes until set on the underside. Transfer to a preheated broiler and cook for 2 to 3 minutes until the top is set and spotted brown. Remove from the heat, let cool, and serve at room temperature.

Many kinds of bread can be used in these fantastic, fresh-tasting pizzas, so don't go shopping specially for ciabatta. You can also use blue cheese, Monterey Jack, or Cheddar instead of mozzarella.

toasted ciabatta pizzas

1 loaf ciabatta, split lengthwise or sliced

1 garlic clove, peeled

about ¼ cup olive oil

4 ripe tomatoes, peeled and sliced

a handful of pitted olives

a bunch of marjoram

10 oz. mozzarella cheese

a bunch of basil

sea salt and freshly ground black pepper

a baking tray

serves 4

Broil the ciabatta under a hot broiler until lightly toasted, then rub with garlic, using it like a grater. Put the garlic ciabatta on a baking tray and drizzle with a little of the olive oil.

Arrange the sliced tomatoes on the bread, then add the olives, marjoram, mozzarella, basil, salt, and pepper. Drizzle some more oil over the top.

Cook in a preheated oven at 350°F for 15 to 20 minutes, until the tomatoes are softened and crisp around the edges and the mozzarella has melted. Remove from the oven, let cool, and wrap in waxed paper before packing.

This quick and simple salad sparkles with the good, clean, peppery taste of salad greens and the delicious crunch of radish and celery.

summer salad

2½ cups watercress, ends trimmed, arugula, or mesclun

a bunch of radishes, trimmed and halved, about 10

6 celery stalks, sliced

¼ cup olive oil

2 tablespoons balsamic vinegar

sea salt and freshly ground black pepper

serves 4

Put the salad greens in a plastic container, then add the halved radishes and sliced celery.

Put the olive oil, vinegar, and salt and pepper to taste in a screw-top jar. When ready to serve, shake the dressing well, then drizzle over the salad. Toss well and serve.

note Some salad items are not good travelers and by the time they make it from your shopping basket to the table, they may have seen better days. Replace any of the ingredients in the above salad with whatever is fresh and best in the market on the day: remember shopping should always be flexible.

Orzo is a rice-shaped pasta, ideal for making into a salad because it retains its shape and texture really well when cooked.

orzo salad
with lemon and herb dressing

2 cups cherry tomatoes, cut in half

⅓ cup extra virgin olive oil

8 oz. orzo or other tiny soup pasta*

6 scallions, finely chopped

¼ cup coarsely chopped mixed fresh herbs, such as basil, dill, mint, and parsley

grated zest and juice of 2 unwaxed lemons

sea salt and freshly ground black pepper

4 wooden skewers, soaked in cold water for 30 minutes

serves 4

Thread the tomatoes onto the soaked wooden skewers with all the cut halves facing the same way. Sprinkle over a little olive oil and season with salt and pepper. Broil under a preheated hot broiler for 1 to 2 minutes on each side until lightly charred and softened.

Bring a large saucepan of lightly salted water to a boil. Add the orzo and cook for about 9 minutes or until *al dente*. Drain well and transfer to a large bowl.

Heat 2 tablespoons of the olive oil in a skillet, add the onions, herbs, and lemon zest, and stir-fry for 30 seconds. Add the mixture to the orzo, then add the tomatoes, lemon juice, remaining olive oil, salt, and pepper. Toss well and let cool before using.

note Orzo is available at most large supermarkets. If unavailable, use other pasta shapes, such as ditalini or pennetti instead.

chicken and tarragon pesto pasta

2½ cups dried penne pasta

½ cup olive oil

1 cup freshly grated Parmesan cheese

½ cup pan-toasted pine nuts

a large bunch of tarragon, leaves stripped from the stem and chopped

grated zest and juice of 1 unwaxed lemon

1 garlic clove, crushed and chopped

3 cooked chicken breast portions, sliced

2 packages fresh arugula, about 1 cup

sea salt and freshly ground black pepper

serves 4

This really is a great dish—tarragon and chicken go together so well. Kids will love it, yet it tastes good enough for adults to tuck into as well. Pesto can be made out of most herbs, so don't hesitate to try your favorites in this recipe and blend to create your own version.

Bring a large saucepan of water to a boil. Add the pasta, stir, and cook for about 10 minutes, until *al dente*. Drain and refresh the pasta in cold water, then drain thoroughly and toss in half the olive oil.

Put the Parmesan, pine nuts, tarragon, lemon zest and juice, garlic, and remaining oil in a bowl and work until smooth with a stick blender.

Put the pasta, pesto, chicken, and arugula in a serving bowl, season with salt and pepper, and toss well, coating the pasta and chicken evenly with the pesto. Serve.

notes When taking this salad on a picnic, don't add the arugula until just before eating or the oil will make it wilt.

If you don't want meat, replace the chicken with steamed vegetables such as zucchini, sugar snap peas, fava beans, or green beans.

This salad has traveled all over the world and many additions to the basic lettuce and croutons with cheese and anchovy dressing can be found. Transforming the salad into a wrap makes a great idea for a picnic dish.

chicken caesar wrap

3 large strips of bacon

8 oz. cooked chicken breast

6 small flour tortillas

1 large romaine lettuce, shredded (inner leaves only)

12 anchovy fillets in oil, drained and chopped

caesar dressing

1 egg yolk

1 tablespoon freshly squeezed lemon juice

1 teaspoon Worcestershire sauce

½ cup olive oil

¼ cup freshly grated Parmesan cheese

sea salt and freshly ground black pepper

serves 6

Broil or sauté the bacon for 2 to 3 minutes until crisp. Let cool, then cut into thin strips. Shred the chicken into large strips.

To make the dressing, put the egg yolk in a small bowl, add the lemon juice, Worcestershire sauce, and a little salt and pepper, and beat until frothy. Gradually beat in the oil, a little at a time, until thickened and glossy. Add 2 tablespoons water to thin the sauce, then stir in the cheese.

Lay one tortilla flat on a counter and arrange a little lettuce down the middle of it. Top with chicken, bacon, anchovies, a spoonful of the dressing, then, more lettuce. Wrap the tortilla into a roll, then wrap the roll in a napkin. Repeat to make 6 wraps. Chill in the refrigerator to serve later.

tiger shrimp
with herb mayonnaise

2 lb. cooked
tiger shrimp

lemon wedges, to serve

herb mayonnaise

2 egg yolks

1 tablespoon freshly
squeezed lemon juice

1 teaspoon Dijon
mustard

1¼ cups olive oil

¼ cup chopped mixed
fresh herbs, such as
basil, chives, chervil, dill,
parsley, and tarragon

sea salt and freshly
ground black pepper

serves 6

Summer and picnics are all about this type of
simple, delicious, messy food. Peel big, juicy,
cooked shrimp, then dunk them into a bowl
of wonderful homemade herb mayonnaise.
Use a plain olive oil, rather than extra virgin,
for mayonnaise, or it can be rather bitter.

To make the mayonnaise, put the egg yolks, lemon
juice, mustard, and a little salt and pepper in a food
processor and blend briefly until frothy. With the
motor running, slowly pour the oil through the feed
tube to make a thick, glossy sauce. If it becomes too
thick, thin it with a little warm water. Add the chopped
herbs and blend again until the mayonnaise is a
vibrant speckled green.

Peel the shrimp and serve with the mayonnaise and
wedges of lemon.

vegetables & vegetarian dishes

grilled corn
with chile-salt rub

*6 ears of corn, husks
removed and ends trimmed*

*2 tablespoons extra virgin
olive oil, plus extra to serve*

3 ancho peppers

1½ tablespoons sea salt

3 limes, cut into wedges

serves 6

One of the Southwest's most popular chiles
is the ancho, the dried version of the poblano.
When ground to a fine powder, it has a smoky
flavor and is mild to medium on the heat scale—
delicious with the sweet, nutty taste of corn.

Bring a large saucepan of lightly salted water to a boil,
add the corn, and boil for 5 minutes. Drain and refresh
under cold water. Pat dry.

Preheat an outdoor grill or broiler until hot. Brush the
corn with oil and cook on the grill or under the broiler for
6 to 8 minutes, turning frequently until charred all over.

Meanwhile, remove the stalk and seeds from the dried
chile peppers. Chop the flesh coarsely and, using a spice
grinder or mortar and pestle, grind to a powder. Transfer
to a small bowl, then mix in the salt.

Rub the lime wedges vigorously over the corn, sprinkle
with the chile salt, and serve with extra oil for drizzling.

If you can find them, use the little Asian eggplants to make this dish—they look very pretty and have a more interesting texture than large eggplants. When buying herbs, try going to independent stores or market stalls where they are sold like bunches of flowers—these herbs taste better and are much better value.

baked eggplants
with pesto sauce

10 oz. small eggplants
¼ cup olive oil
basil pesto (page 228)*

a baking tray, lightly oiled

serves 4

Cut the eggplants in half lengthwise and put on the baking tray. Drizzle with a little of the olive oil and cook in a preheated oven at 375°F for about 20 minutes, then turn them over and cook for a further 15 minutes.

To make the pesto, put the basil, pine nuts, garlic, Parmesan, the remaining olive oil, and salt and pepper in a blender and purée until smooth. When the eggplants are cooked, drizzle with the pesto and serve hot or cold.

*note Make twice the quantity of pesto and store the extra in the refrigerator—it always comes in handy as an easy salad dressing or tossed through pasta for a quick, delicious supper. Keep the pesto covered with a thin film of olive oil and it will stay fresh for several weeks.

If you can find it, use purple basil, which looks even more spectacular than green. This dish really couldn't be easier, and makes a nice change from roasted tomato halves.

mozzarella baked tomatoes

20 ripe tomatoes

8 oz. mozzarella cheese, drained and cut into 20 pieces

½ cup olive oil

a bunch of fresh basil leaves, torn

sea salt and freshly ground black pepper

a large baking tray, lightly oiled

serves 20

Cut a deep cross, to about halfway down, in the top of each tomato and push a piece of mozzarella into each one. Transfer to the baking tray and sprinkle with salt and pepper.

Cook in a preheated oven at 325°F for 25 minutes until the tomatoes are beginning to soften and open up.

Sprinkle with oil and basil and serve warm.

Basil oil is particularly good sprinkled onto this simple tart, but you can use ordinary olive oil. Preheating the baking tray will make the base of the tart beautifully crisp.

simple tomato and olive tart
with basil oil

12 oz. ready-made puff pastry dough, thawed if frozen

4 oz. red cherry tomatoes, cut in half

8 oz. yellow cherry tomatoes, cut in half

½ cup semi-dried or sun-dried tomatoes, cut in half

½ cup black olives, such as Niçoise or Kalamata, pitted and cut in half

⅓ cup freshly grated Parmesan cheese

sea salt and freshly ground black pepper

a handful of arugula, to serve

basil oil

½ cup fresh basil leaves

⅔ cup extra virgin olive oil

a pinch of sea salt

2 baking trays

serves 4

To make the basil oil, blanch the leaves very briefly in boiling water, drain, and dry thoroughly with paper towels. Put in a blender, add the oil and salt, and blend until very smooth. Pour the oil through a fine strainer, or one lined with cheesecloth. Keep in the refrigerator but return to room temperature before using.

Preheat the oven to 425°F and put a baking tray on the middle shelf to heat up.

Roll out the dough on a lightly floured surface to form a rectangle, 10 x 12 inches. Trim the edges and transfer the dough to a second baking tray. Using the blade of a sharp knife, gently tap the edges several times (this will help the dough rise and the edges separate) and prick all over with a fork.

Put the tomatoes, olives, basil oil, salt, and pepper in a bowl and mix lightly. Spoon the mixture over the dough and carefully slide the tart directly onto the preheated baking tray. Bake for 12 to 15 minutes until risen and golden.

Remove from the oven and sprinkle with the Parmesan. Cut into four and serve hot with a handful of arugula.

Experiment with different fillings, for instance use sun-dried bell peppers in place of the tomatoes.

zucchini quiche

Put all the pastry dough ingredients in a food processor and blend until the ingredients just come together. Invert the mixture onto a lightly floured counter and bring it together with your hands. Pat into a disk, wrap, and chill it for 20 minutes.

Put the dough on a lightly floured counter and roll out to a disk just bigger than the tart pan. Line the tart pan with it and cut off excess dough from the edges. Chill for 15 minutes.

Line the tart shell with wax paper and fill with baking beans or uncooked rice. Bake in a preheated oven at 400°F for 10 to 15 minutes, then remove the wax paper and beans and return the tart shell to the oven for a further 3 to 5 minutes until just cooked. Remove from the oven and reduce the oven to 350°F.

To make the filling, put a few drops of the oil in a skillet and wipe it over the surface with a paper towel. Heat until hot, add the zucchini, and sauté in batches until golden on both sides.

Put the crème fraîche or sour cream in a bowl, add the whole eggs and yolks, and beat to mix. Add salt and pepper to taste. Arrange the zucchini slices in the cooked tart shell, add the sun-dried tomatoes, then pour in the egg mixture. Bake in the preheated oven for 30 to 35 minutes until golden and set. Serve hot, warm, or cold.

pastry dough

1¾ cups plus 2 tablespoons all-purpose flour, plus extra for dusting

a pinch of salt

1 stick plus 3 tablespoons chilled butter, diced

2 large egg yolks

3–4 tablespoons very cold water

filling

2 tablespoons olive oil

1½ lb. zucchini, sliced diagonally

1⅓ cups crème fraîche or sour cream

2 whole eggs, plus 2 egg yolks

5–6 pieces sun-dried tomatoes in olive oil, drained and coarsely chopped

sea salt and freshly ground black pepper

a loose-base tart pan, 10 inches diameter

wax paper and baking beans or uncooked rice

serves 8

fish, meat, & poultry

Meat and fish (the old-fashioned surf 'n' turf)
can work well together and this recipe is a
perfect example of this balance of strong flavors.
This recipe uses the chorizo sausage that needs
cooking, rather than the cured tapas variety,
although either would do.

shrimp, chorizo, and sage skewers

10 oz. uncooked chorizo

*24 large, uncooked, peeled
shrimp, deveined*

24 large fresh sage leaves

extra virgin olive oil

freshly squeezed lemon juice

freshly ground black pepper

12 skewers, metal or bamboo
(if using bamboo, soak them in
warm water for 30 minutes)

serves 6

Cut the chorizo into 24 slices about ½ inch thick and
thread onto the skewers, alternating with the shrimp and
sage leaves. Put a little oil and lemon juice in a small bowl
or pitcher, mix well, then drizzle over the skewers. Sprinkle
with pepper.

Meanwhile, preheat an overhead broiler, stove-top
grill pan, or outdoor grill until hot. Cook the skewers
for 1½ to 2 minutes on each side until the chorizo and
shrimp are cooked through. Serve at once.

The squid will curl up as they cook, so use a pair of tongs to open them out again and press them flat. You could also put a heatproof plate on top to keep them that way. Take care not to overcook squid or it will be tough.

seared squid with lemon and cilantro dressing

4 medium squid, cleaned*, about 1½ lb.

1 tablespoon extra virgin olive oil

sea salt and freshly ground black pepper

baby spinach leaves, to serve

lemon and cilantro dressing

5⅓ cup peanut oil

1 tablespoon toasted sesame oil

freshly squeezed juice of 1 lemon

2 tablespoons sweet soy sauce, (Indonesian kecap manis), or regular soy sauce with ½ teaspoon sugar added

2 tablespoons chopped fresh cilantro

1 garlic clove, crushed

serves 4

To make the dressing, put the ingredients in a screw-top bottle, shake well, and use as required. If storing in the refrigerator, omit the cilantro, and add just before use.

Cut the squid bodies in half and open out flat. Brush with the olive oil and season with salt and pepper.

Heat a stove-top grill pan for 5 minutes until very hot. Add the squid bodies and tentacles and cook for 1 minute on each side until charred and tender. Transfer to a board and cut the squid into thick slices.

Put the dressing in a bowl, add the squid, and toss well. Serve with a few baby spinach leaves and extra black pepper.

*note Squid is very easy to clean. Pull out the tentacles (the insides should come with them). Cut off the tentacles and discard the insides. Rinse out the bodies, pulling out the stiff transparent quill, like a little wand of plastic. Use the bodies and tentacles. That's it.

salmon frittata
with potatoes and asparagus

A frittata is an Italian omelet cooked slowly over low heat, with the filling stirred into the eggs or spread over the top. It is served perfectly set, never folded, and makes a terrific lunchtime snack or party food.

8 oz. fresh asparagus, trimmed

6 oz. small new potatoes

6 eggs, preferably farm-fresh

½ cup freshly grated Parmesan cheese

3 tablespoons chopped fresh mixed herbs, such as parsley, tarragon, and chervil

3 tablespoons butter

8 oz. fresh salmon, skinned and diced into large chunks

sea salt and freshly ground black pepper

a heavy, nonstick skillet, 9 inches diameter

serves 2–4

Steam the asparagus for 12 minutes, or until tender, plunge into cold water to set the color and cool completely.

Cook the potatoes in boiling salted water for 15 to 20 minutes until tender. Drain, let cool, then slice thickly. Drain the asparagus, then dry it and cut into short lengths.

Beat the eggs in a bowl with a pinch of salt, lots of pepper, and half the Parmesan. Stir in the asparagus and herbs. Melt the butter in the skillet. When foaming, pour in the egg mixture, then sprinkle the salmon all over. Turn down the heat as low as possible. Cook for about 15 minutes until set, but with the top still a little runny.

Arrange the cooked sliced potato on top and sprinkle with the remaining Parmesan. Cook under a hot broiler until the cheese is lightly browned and the top is just set—it should not brown too much or it will dry out.

Slide onto a warm plate, cut into 4 wedges, and serve.

If you find some really fresh swordfish at the market, try this recipe. It is easy to overcook swordfish, which will become tough, so follow the timings below and err on the side of caution—you can always put the fish back on the heat for a moment or two longer if necessary.

seared swordfish
with new potatoes, beans, and olives

Brush the swordfish steaks with 1 tablespoon of the oil, season with salt and pepper, and set aside.

To make the dressing, put the remaining oil in a bowl, add the lemon juice, sugar, chives, salt, and pepper, beat well, and set aside.

Cook the potatoes in a saucepan of lightly salted boiling water for 10 minutes, add the beans, and cook for a further 3 to 4 minutes, or until the potatoes and beans are just tender. Drain well. Transfer to a bowl, add the olives and half the dressing, and toss well.

Cook the swordfish steaks on a preheated outdoor grill or stove-top grill pan for about 1½ minutes on each side. Let rest in a warm oven for 5 minutes. Sprinkle the swordfish with the remaining dressing and the balsamic vinegar and serve with the warm potato salad.

4 swordfish steaks, 8 oz. each

½ cup extra virgin olive oil

2 tablespoons freshly squeezed lemon juice

½ teaspoon sugar

1 tablespoon fresh chives, snipped

1 lb. new potatoes, cut in half if large

8 oz. string beans, trimmed

½ cup black olives, such as Niçoise or Kalamata, pitted and chopped

sea salt and freshly ground black pepper

1 tablespoon Reduced Balsamic Vinegar (page 147), to serve

serves 4

This marinade is typical of Japanese cooking and imparts a really fantastic flavor to the fish. Miso is a fermented soybean-based paste, available in Asian stores, gourmet food stores, and larger supermarkets. As a guide, the lighter the color, the sweeter the flavor.

broiled miso cod

3 tablespoons Japanese
soy sauce (shoyu)

3 tablespoons sake

3 tablespoons honey

2 tablespoons
miso paste

6 cod fillets, 8 oz. each

to serve

pickled ginger

stir-fried baby bok choy

steamed rice

serves 6

Put the soy sauce, sake, honey, and miso in a small saucepan and heat gently until smooth. Set aside to cool completely. Pour into a shallow dish, add the cod fillets, cover, and let marinate in the refrigerator for at least 4 hours.

Return to room temperature for 1 hour before cooking. Transfer the fillets to a broiler pan lined with foil and cook under a preheated broiler for 4 minutes on each side, basting halfway through. Let rest for 5 minutes, then serve with pickled ginger, stir-fried bok choy, and rice.

In Greece, stifado (or *stifatho*) can refer to a number of things, but essentially it is a thickened stew with tomato and garlic and olive oil. Sometimes made with beef or rabbit, guinea fowl, or even quail, it is a handsome dish, easy to prepare, and fragrant with herbs. The flambé is an unusual touch–optional, but fun. Serve from the dish, accompanied with country bread, noodles, rice, or even French fries.

greek chicken stifado

3 lb. chicken, whole or cut into 4 pieces, or 4 breast or leg portions

2 tablespoons extra virgin olive oil

10 whole cloves

20 pearl onions or 10 shallots, cut in half

8–12 canned baby artichokes, drained

4 garlic cloves, chopped

2 tablespoons white wine vinegar or freshly squeezed lemon juice

⅓ cup rich tomato paste (double strength)

14 oz. canned chopped tomatoes

24 black olives, such as Kalamata

a large bunch of fresh or dried rosemary, oregano, thyme, or a mixture

2 tablespoons Greek Metaxa brandy (optional)

freshly ground black pepper

serves 4

Pat the chicken dry with paper towels. Heat the olive oil in a large flameproof casserole dish, add the chicken, and sauté for 8 to 10 minutes, turning it with tongs from time to time.

Push the cloves into some of the onions and add them all to the pan. Add the artichokes, garlic, vinegar, tomato paste, canned tomatoes, olives, and black pepper. Tuck in the herb sprigs around the edges.

Bring to a boil and reduce the heat to low. Cover and simmer for 30 minutes, or about 60 minutes if using a whole bird–or until the chicken seems tender and the sauce has reduced and thickened.

Heat the brandy in a warmed ladle and pour it, flaming, over the stifado. Serve immediately.

In a simple dish such as this, quality ingredients are important. Choose an organic or free-range chicken, unwaxed lemons, a good Modena balsamic vinegar, and extra virgin oil. It really makes a difference.

rosemary and lemon roasted chicken

4 lb. chicken pieces

3 lemons, cut into wedges

leaves from a large bunch of rosemary

3 red onions

¾ cup large black olives (about 10–12), pitted

¼ cup balsamic vinegar

2 tablespoons extra virgin olive oil

sea salt and freshly ground black pepper

a large roasting pan

serves 4

Trim off any excess fat from the chicken pieces and put them in a large bowl. Add the lemons and rosemary.

Cut the onions in half lengthwise, leaving the root end intact. Cut the halves into wedges and add to the chicken.

Add the olives, balsamic vinegar, olive oil, and salt and pepper, and mix well to coat the chicken with the flavorings.

Cover and let stand at room temperature for 1 hour, or in the refrigerator overnight.

Put the chicken in a large roasting pan and spoon the marinade around it. Cook in a preheated oven at 375°F for 30 minutes. Turn the chicken pieces in the pan for even cooking and coloring, then cook for a further 30 minutes.

Remove the chicken from the oven. Using a slotted spoon, lift out the chicken, lemons, onions, and olives and put them on a serving dish. Skim the cooking juices, discarding the fat. Pour the juices over the chicken and serve hot or at room temperature.

orange and soy glazed duck

This is a great dish when you are short of time—it is quick to cook and tastes delicious. Serve the duck breasts with your choice of vegetables such as steamed napa cabbage, bok choy, steamed broccoli, or sautéed spinach.

4 duck breast fillets, about 8 oz. each

freshly squeezed juice of 1 orange

3 tablespoons dark soy sauce

2 tablespoons maple syrup

½ teaspoon Chinese five-spice powder

2 garlic cloves, crushed

freshly ground Szechuan peppercorns or black pepper

to serve

steamed broccoli, bok choy, or sautéed spinach

1 orange, cut into wedges

serves 4

Using a sharp knife, score the fat on each duck breast crosswise several times, then put the breasts in a shallow dish.

Put the orange juice, soy sauce, maple syrup, five-spice powder, garlic, and pepper in a small pitcher or bowl, mix well, then pour the mixture over the duck fillets. Cover with plastic wrap and marinate in the refrigerator for as long as possible. You can leave them overnight, but let them return to room temperature for 1 hour before cooking.

Heat a stove-top grill pan until hot, add the duck breasts, skin side down, and sear for 1 to 2 minutes. Transfer to a roasting pan, adding the marinade juices. Cook the duck in a preheated oven at 400°F for about 10 minutes, or until medium rare. Remove the duck from the oven, wrap it in foil, and keep it warm for 5 minutes.

Pour the juices from the roasting pan into a small saucepan and, using a large spoon, very carefully skim the fat off the surface. Heat the juices to boiling point and boil for 2 minutes, until thickened slightly. Serve the duck breasts sprinkled with the juices and accompanied with the broccoli, bok choy, or spinach and orange wedges.

This is probably the best way to cook lamb on the grill—the bone is removed and the meat opened out flat so it can cook quickly and evenly. Ask the butcher to bone the lamb for you.

butterflied lamb
with white bean salad

Put the lamb in a shallow dish, pour the marinade over the top, cover, and let marinate in the refrigerator overnight. Remove from the refrigerator 1 hour before cooking.

To make the salsa verde, put all the ingredients except the oil in a food processor and blend to a smooth paste. Gradually pour the oil through the feed tube to form a sauce, then taste and adjust the seasoning, if necessary.

To make the salad, put the onion in a colander, sprinkle with salt, and let drain over a bowl for 30 minutes. Wash the onion under cold running water and dry well. Transfer to a bowl, then add the beans, garlic, tomatoes, olive oil, vinegar, parsley, and salt and pepper to taste.

Preheat the barbecue. Drain the lamb and discard the marinade. Cook over medium-hot coals for 12 to 15 minutes on each side until charred on the outside but still pink in the middle (cook for a little longer if you prefer the meat less rare). Let the lamb rest for 10 minutes. Cut the lamb into slices and serve with the bean salad and salsa verde.

3–4 lb. leg of lamb, butterflied

1 recipe Herb, Lemon, and Garlic Marinade (page 235)

white bean salad

1 large red onion, finely chopped

3 cans white or cannellini beans, drained, 15½ oz. each

2 garlic cloves, chopped

3 tomatoes, seeded and chopped

⅓ cup extra virgin olive oil

1½ tablespoons red wine vinegar

2 tablespoons chopped fresh parsley

sea salt and freshly ground black pepper

salsa verde

a large bunch of fresh parsley

a small bunch of mixed fresh herbs such as basil, chives, and mint

1 garlic clove, chopped

1 tablespoon pitted green olives

1 tablespoon capers, drained and washed

2 anchovy fillets, washed and chopped

1 teaspoon Dijon mustard

2 teaspoons white wine vinegar

⅔ cup extra virgin olive oil

serves 8

souvlaki in pita

4 large pita breads

water and olive oil, to moisten
the bread

2 teaspoons chopped fresh
oregano, or 1 teaspoon dried
oregano, crushed

2 tablespoons freshly squeezed
lemon juice

½ onion, coarsely grated

2 tablespoons extra virgin olive oil

1 lb. lean pork or lamb (usually
leg meat), cut into ½-inch cubes

salad, such as

lettuce or cabbage, thinly sliced

cucumber, sliced

red bell pepper, sliced

tomatoes, cut into wedges

radishes, cut in half

red onion, sliced into rings

garlic dressing

⅓ cup plain yogurt, drained

4 garlic cloves, crushed

2 inches cucumber, coarsely
grated, then squeezed dry

½ teaspoon sea salt

metal skewers

serves 4

Souvlaki is the Greek equivalent of the kabob, a street food traditionally eaten at festival time. These days, it is mostly made of pork (although lamb is used when in season). Loved by locals and travelers alike, it is inexpensive, filling, and delicious.

Brush or sprinkle the pita breads all over with the water and oil and either broil or bake in a preheated oven at 350°F for 3 to 5 minutes or long enough to soften the bread, but not dry it. Cut off a strip from the long side, then pull open and part the sides of the breads to make a pocket. Push the strip inside. Keep the breads warm.

Put the oregano, lemon juice, onion, and olive oil in a bowl and mash with a fork. Add the cubed meat and toss well. Cover and let marinate for 10 to 20 minutes. Drain, then thread the meat onto metal skewers. Cook on a preheated outdoor grill or stove-top grill pan for 5 to 8 minutes, or until golden outside and cooked through.

Put your choice of salad ingredients in a bowl, toss gently, then insert into the pockets of the pita breads.

To make the dressing, put the yogurt in a bowl, then beat in the garlic, cucumber, and salt. Add a large spoonful to each pocket.

Remove the hot, cooked meat from the skewers, then push it into the pockets. Serve immediately, while the meat and bread are hot and the salad cool.

pasta, pizza, & rice

This sauce is best made as soon as the new season's tomatoes arrive in the stores, especially the vine-ripened varieties that we see more and more. If you don't cook with gas, then simply plunge the tomatoes in boiling water for 1 minute, drain, refresh, and peel off the skin.

pasta with fresh tomato

2 lb. ripe tomatoes

⅓ cup extra virgin olive oil

2 fresh red chiles, seeded and chopped

2 garlic cloves, crushed

a bunch of basil, chopped

1 teaspoon sugar

12 oz. dried spaghetti

sea salt and freshly ground black pepper

freshly grated pecorino or Parmesan cheese, to serve (optional)

serves 4

Holding each tomato with tongs or a skewer, char them over a gas flame, until the skins blister and start to shrivel. Peel off the skins, chop the flesh, and put in a bowl. Add the oil, chiles, garlic, basil, sugar, salt, and pepper and leave to steep while you cook the pasta (or longer if possible).

Bring a large saucepan of water to a boil. Add a pinch of salt, then the pasta, and cook for about 10 minutes until *al dente*, or according to the instructions on the package. Drain well and immediately stir in the fresh tomato sauce. Serve at once with the grated cheese, if using.

Wide ribbon pasta is particularly popular in Tuscany and also in Umbria. Frequently, it is served with rich meat and game sauces, but freshly made basil oil dressing is a superb summery alternative. Eat this dish on its own or use it as an accompaniment.

pappardelle with basil oil

14 oz. dried pappardelle (wide pasta ribbons), plain or frilly edged

⅓ cup extra virgin olive oil

2 garlic cloves, chopped

a handful of fresh chives, chervil, dill, or parsley, plus extra to serve (optional)

2 large handfuls of fresh basil leaves

¼ cup slivered almonds

¼ cup freshly grated pecorino or Parmesan cheese

sea salt and freshly ground black pepper

lemon wedges, to serve (optional)

serves 4

Bring a large saucepan of water to a boil. Add a large pinch of salt, then the pappardelle, and cook for about 10 minutes until *al dente*, or according to the instructions on the package.

Meanwhile, heat half the oil in a skillet, add the garlic, chives, and one handful of the basil leaves. Sauté for 1 to 1½ minutes, or until the greens have wilted and the garlic is aromatic.

Transfer to a small food processor and blend to a paste. Alternatively, transfer to a mortar and pound with a pestle. Pour into a plastic or stainless steel (non-reactive) strainer set over a bowl. Press all the oil through with the back of a ladle or wooden spoon.

Heat the remaining olive oil in the skillet, add the almonds, and sauté, until golden.

Drain the cooked pasta, add it to the skillet with the almonds, the basil oil, and the remaining basil leaves, the cheese, and extra chives, if using. Add salt and pepper to taste and serve hot or warm, with lemon wedges, if using.

variation Alternatively, don't strain the basil mixture—just stir it through the cooked pasta and proceed as in the main recipe.

slow-roasted tomatoes
with ricotta and spaghetti

6 large, ripe tomatoes, cut in half

4 sprigs of oregano, plus
2 tablespoons chopped
fresh oregano

½ cup extra virgin olive oil

1 lb. spaghetti

4 garlic cloves, sliced

1 dried red chile pepper, such as
ancho or New Mexico, chopped

freshly squeezed juice of ½ lemon

1 cup fresh ricotta cheese,
crumbled into big pieces

sea salt and freshly ground
black pepper

freshly grated Parmesan cheese,
to serve

serves 4

A pasta dish full of the flavors of the Mediterranean.
Roast the tomatoes ahead of time, if you like, then
reheat at 350°F for 15 minutes.

Put the tomatoes cut side up in a shallow roasting pan. Sprinkle
with the sprigs of oregano, 1 tablespoon of the oil, and lots of salt
and pepper. Roast in a preheated oven at 475°F for 20 minutes.
Reduce to 300°F and cook for a further 1 to 1½ hours, until the
tomatoes are golden, glossy, and reduced in size by about one-
third. Remove from the oven and keep them warm.

Bring a large saucepan of water to a boil. Add a large pinch of salt,
then the spaghetti, and return to a boil. Cook for about 10 minutes
until al dente, or according to the instructions on the package.

After about 5 minutes, put the remaining oil in a large, deep
skillet, heat well, add the garlic, and sauté gently for 2 minutes
until softened but not golden. Add the chile pepper and cook
for 1 minute more.

Drain the cooked pasta, reserving ¼ cup of the cooking liquid. Add
the pasta and reserved water to the skillet, then add the chopped
oregano, lemon juice, salt, and pepper. Toss over the heat for
about 2 minutes. Serve the pasta topped with the tomatoes,
ricotta, and a light dusting of grated Parmesan.

You can use store-bought fresh pasta, but have a go at making it yourself: you really will notice the difference. This one is flavored with dill and black pepper—really punchy with rich smoky salmon and the sharpness of lemon butter sauce.

smoked salmon in lemon cream sauce with dill tagliatelle

To make the pasta, sift the flour and salt onto a board and make a well in the center. Put the eggs, oil, black pepper, and dill in a food processor and blend until smooth. Pour into the well in the flour and gradually mix into the flour, bringing the dough together. Knead for 5 to 10 minutes, until smooth. Wrap, then let rest at room temperature for 30 minutes.

Using a pasta machine, roll the dough into sheets, then cut into tagliatelle—strips about ½ inch wide. Hang up to dry slightly or arrange on clean dish cloths dusted with semolina flour.

Cut the smoked salmon into strips, cover, and set aside.

To make the sauce, put the lemon zest, cream, and fish stock in a saucepan, bring to a boil, then remove from the heat and steep for 15 minutes. Remove and discard the lemon zest, then boil the sauce rapidly until it has slightly thickened and reduced.

Bring a large saucepan of water to a boil. Add a large pinch of salt, then the tagliatelle and stir well. Return to a boil—when the water is boiling again, the pasta is cooked. Drain well and quickly toss with the sauce and smoked salmon. Transfer to warm bowls, sprinkle with chopped dill, and serve immediately.

8 oz. smoked salmon

sea salt

chopped fresh dill, to serve

fresh pasta

2 cups white bread flour or all-purpose flour

½ teaspoon salt

3 large eggs

1 tablespoon olive oil

1 tablespoon freshly ground black pepper (very finely ground)

1½ cups (2 oz.) fresh dill sprigs

fine semolina flour, for dusting (optional)

lemon cream sauce

zest of 2 unwaxed lemons

1¼ cups heavy cream

⅔ cup well-flavored fish stock

a pasta machine

serves 4

chile tuna tartare pasta

"Tartare" means uncooked and, to serve fish this way, you must use very fresh, sashimi-grade tuna. If you prefer your tuna cooked, sear it on a preheated stove-top grill pan for 1 minute on each side, or until cooked to your liking. However, do try it tartare—it is delicious, as the Japanese well know.

12 oz. dried fusilli or other pasta

⅓ cup extra virgin olive oil, plus extra for serving

4 garlic cloves, sliced

1–2 dried red chiles, seeded and chopped

grated zest and juice of 1 unwaxed lemon

1 tablespoon chopped fresh thyme leaves

1 lb. tuna steak, chopped

a handful of fresh basil leaves

sea salt and freshly ground black pepper

serves 4

Bring a large saucepan of water to a boil. Add a large pinch of salt, then the pasta, and return to a boil. Cook for about 10 minutes until *al dente*, or according to the instructions on the package.

Meanwhile, heat the oil in a skillet, add the garlic, and sauté gently for 2 minutes, until lightly golden. Add the chile, lemon zest, and thyme and sauté for 1 minute more.

Drain the pasta, reserving ¼ cup of the cooking liquid, and return both to the pan. Stir in the hot garlic oil mixture, lemon juice, raw tuna, basil leaves, salt and pepper, and a little extra olive oil. Serve immediately.

Vary the seafood depending on what's available and best on the day, but always include clams or mussels—for their flavor as well as their beautiful shells.

seafood spaghettini

10 oz. dried pasta, such as spaghettini

¼ cup olive oil

1 garlic clove, finely chopped

10 oz. mixed seafood, such as squid, cut into rings, peeled shrimp, and scallops, shells removed and cut in half crosswise

1 lb. fresh mussels or clams in shells, scrubbed

2 tablespoons chopped fresh flat-leaf parsley

sea salt and freshly ground black pepper

serves 4

Bring a large saucepan of water to a boil. Add a good pinch of salt, then the pasta, and cook for about 10 minutes until *al dente*, or according to the instructions on the package.

Meanwhile, heat half the oil in a large sauté pan or saucepan. Add the mixed seafood and cook for 3 to 4 minutes, stirring constantly, until just cooked. Transfer to a large bowl and set aside.

Add the mussels or clams to the seafood pan, cover with a lid, and cook for 5 minutes until all the shells have opened, discarding any that remain closed.

Drain the pasta well and return it to the warm pan. Add the mussels or clams, seafood, remaining olive oil, and parsley. Add salt and pepper to taste, toss gently, then serve.

This is similar to the Italian "calzone" or stuffed pizza. They are often available at Turkish food stalls, where the chefs busily knead, roll, and cook these delicious pizzas.

turkish pizza turnover

3 cups white bread flour, plus extra for kneading

1½ teaspoons active dry yeast

1½ teaspoons sea salt

1 tablespoon extra virgin olive oil

filling

1 lb. spinach leaves

1 tablespoon extra virgin olive oil

1 small onion, finely chopped

2 garlic cloves, crushed

4 oz. feta cheese, crumbled

2 tablespoons grated Parmesan cheese

2 tablespoons mascarpone cheese

a little grated nutmeg

freshly ground black pepper

serves 4

Sift the flour into the bowl of an electric mixer with dough hook attachment. Alternatively, use a food processor with a plastic blade attachment. Stir in the yeast and salt. Add the oil and ½ to ⅔ cup warm water and work until the dough is smooth and elastic.

Meanwhile, to make the filling, discard any thick spinach stalks, then wash the leaves in a colander. Drain, transfer to a large saucepan, and heat gently for 2 to 3 minutes, until the leaves have wilted. Rinse under cold water, drain completely, and squeeze out as much water as possible. Finely chop the spinach and set aside.

Heat the oil in a skillet, add the onion and garlic, and sauté gently for 5 minutes, until very soft and lightly golden. Stir in the spinach, the cheeses, nutmeg, and pepper, then remove from the heat.

Transfer the dough to a lightly floured surface and knead it gently. Divide the dough into 4 equal pieces and roll out each piece to a rectangle 8 x 16 inches (it will be very thin). Spread one-quarter of the spinach mixture over half the dough, fold over, and seal the edges. Repeat with the other pieces of dough to make 4 turnovers.

Heat the flat plate of an outdoor grill for 5 minutes, then reduce the heat to medium. Brush with a little oil, add the stuffed pizzas, and cook for 4 to 5 minutes on each side, until golden. Alternatively, cook on a flat griddle or large, heavy skillet. Serve hot.

To make pizza at home, it helps to have a pizza stone or flat earthenware tile to bake it on. If not, use a heavy, old, dark, metal baking sheet, which will hold the heat well.

3⅓ cups white bread flour, plus extra for kneading

2 tablespoons sugar

1½ teaspoons salt

1 envelope active dry yeast, ¼ oz.

1⅓ cups lukewarm water

1 egg, beaten

2 tablespoons extra virgin olive oil

topping

14 oz. canned chopped plum tomatoes

2 garlic cloves, chopped

1 tablespoon sugar

¼ cup extra virgin olive oil

a large handful of fresh basil leaves, torn

24 anchovies

24 capers

1 dried red chile, crumbled (optional)

8 oz. mozzarella cheese, sliced (optional)

24 black olives, pitted

1 pizza stone or baking trays

a pizza peel

makes 4

pizza napoletana

Put the flour, sugar, salt, and yeast in a food processor. Pulse a few times to mix and sift. Put the warm water, egg, and olive oil in a bowl and beat well. With the machine running, add the mixture to the processor through the feed tube. The dough will form, clump, then gather in a mass. Remove to a well-floured counter, sprinkle with extra flour, and knead the dough for 2 to 3 minutes, or until smooth and silky.

Put the dough in a lightly oiled bowl and enclose in a large plastic bag. Leave in a warm place until doubled in size, about 1 hour. Remove the dough from the bowl and punch it down. Cut it into 4 pieces. Preheat the pizza stone or baking sheet on the top oven shelf at 425°F, until very hot.

Put the pieces of dough on a well-floured surface and shape into rounds about ½ inch thick, but thicker around the edges. Make indentations with your fingertips all over the surface. Let rise while you make the topping.

Meanwhile, put the tomatoes in a large, shallow saucepan, then add the garlic, sugar, half the oil, and half the basil. Bring to a boil and cook, uncovered, for 8 to 12 minutes, until reduced by half. Use a peel to slide one pizza dough base onto the hot pizza stone. Spread one-quarter of the hot tomato sauce on top leaving 1 inch bare at the edges. Sprinkle with one-quarter of the anchovies, capers, and chile and mozzarella, if using. Return to the oven and bake for 10 to 12 minutes, or until risen, blistered, hot, and fragrant. Top with a few basil leaves, a little oil, and serve hot or warm. Repeat to make 3 more.

This Spanish tart, or *coca*, can be found in tapas bars. Piled hot and high and served with olives and glasses of the local wine, it can be a revelation. If you haven't any piquillo peppers, use canned bell peppers, pimientos, or broiled or roasted fresh red bell peppers.

spanish tart with bell peppers

To make the dough, put the flour, yeast, and salt in a bowl and mix. Add the water and mix to a satiny dough, then knead, still in the bowl, for 5 minutes, or until silky. Cover the bowl with a cloth and leave for about 1 hour, or until the dough has doubled in size.

Meanwhile, to make the topping, heat 3 tablespoons of the oil in a skillet, add the onions, and cook, stirring, over medium heat until softened and transparent. Slice half the peppers and add to the pan. Stir in most of the herbs.

Transfer the dough to a heavy, dark, oiled baking sheet. Punch down, flatten, and roll out the dough to a round 12 inches diameter. Snip, twist, or roll the edges. Spread all over with the anchovy paste. Add the whole bell peppers and the cooked onion mixture. Arrange the anchovies and remaining herbs in a decorative pattern on top and sprinkle with the remaining oil.

Bake in a preheated oven at 425°F for 25 to 30 minutes, until the base is crisp and risen, the edges golden, and the filling hot and wilted. Serve in wedges, hot or cool.

1⅔ cups all-purpose flour

½ envelope active dry yeast, ⅛ oz.

½ teaspoon salt

⅔ cup lukewarm water

topping

¼ cup extra virgin olive oil

2 large red onions, about 12 oz.

about 1 lb. canned sweet red bell peppers, drained

leaves from a small handful of thyme or rosemary sprigs

2 tablespoons anchovy paste, or canned anchovies, chopped and mashed

16 marinated anchovy fillets

a baking tray, oiled

serves 4–6

Although this risotto is best made with fresh peas, you can also use frozen. The mint adds a delicious fresh flavor. This will serve four as an entrée or six as an appetizer.

fresh pea and lettuce risotto

4 tablespoons butter

1 large onion, finely chopped

2 garlic cloves, crushed

1 leek, trimmed and sliced

1½ cups arborio rice

½ cup dry vermouth or fino sherry

1 quart vegetable stock

2¼ cups fresh or frozen peas

4 oz. romaine lettuce leaves, washed and shredded

¼ cup chopped fresh mint leaves, plus extra mint leaves, to serve

¼ cup mascarpone cheese

¾ cup freshly grated Parmesan cheese

sea salt and freshly ground black pepper

serves 4–6

Put the butter in a saucepan, melt gently, then add the onion, garlic, and leek, and sauté gently for 10 minutes, until softened but not golden. Add the rice, stir for 1 minute until all the grains are glossy, then add the vermouth or sherry. Let bubble and evaporate.

Meanwhile, put the stock in a separate saucepan and heat until just barely simmering. Add about ½ cup of the hot vegetable stock to the rice. Add the peas and a little salt and pepper, then stir until the liquid has been absorbed. Continue adding the stock and stirring the rice until almost all the stock has been used. Add the lettuce, chopped mint, and the remaining stock and cook until absorbed.

Remove the pan from the heat, stir in the mascarpone and ½ cup of the Parmesan, and season to taste with salt and pepper. Cover the pan and set aside for 5 minutes before serving, topped with the remaining Parmesan and mint leaves.

This now-grand Spanish rice dish, once a poor man's food from Albufera in Valencia, is made in countless variations in different areas, depending on local ingredients and styles. Use hard, stubby, calasparra rice (sometimes labeled simply "paella rice" in supermarkets) and don't stir it constantly like risotto.

paella

8 chicken drumsticks and thighs, mixed, or 1 whole chicken, about 3 lb., cut into pieces

2 teaspoons sea salt

4 teaspoons smoked paprika or paprika

¼ cup extra virgin olive oil

3–4 boneless pork chops, or 12 oz. salt pork cut into 1-inch cubes

2 onions, chopped

4 garlic cloves, crushed

1 lb. tomatoes, fresh or canned, peeled, seeded, and chopped

2 large pinches of saffron threads, or 3 envelopes ground saffron

1¾ cups calasparra (paella) rice

3–3½ cups boiling chicken stock or water

1 cup shelled fresh peas, or frozen peas, thawed

6 oz. green beans, cut in half

8 baby artichokes, cut in half lengthwise, or canned or marinated equivalent

8 large uncooked shrimp, shell on

freshly ground black pepper

serves 4–6

Pat the chicken dry with paper towels. Put the salt, pepper, and paprika in a bowl and mix well. Sprinkle the chicken with half the mixture and toss well.

Heat the oil in a large, shallow skillet. Add the chicken and pork, in batches if necessary, and sauté over medium heat for 10 to 12 minutes, or until well browned. Remove with a slotted spoon and set aside.

Add the onions, garlic, tomatoes, and saffron to the pan, then add the remaining salt and paprika mixture. Cook until thickened, about 5 minutes. Stir well, then return the meats to the pan and stir in the rice and most of the hot stock. Cook over high heat until bubbling fiercely, then reduce the heat and simmer gently, uncovered, for 15 minutes.

Add the peas, beans, artichokes, shrimp, and remaining stock, if necessary, and continue to cook for 10 to 15 minutes, or until the rice is cooked and glossy but dry. Serve the paella straight from the pan.

grilling

Serving a large platter of grilled vegetables provides a
lovely start to any barbecue party–choose a combination
of your favorites. A delicious way to serve them is on a
bed of grilled polenta.

vegetable antipasti

2 red bell peppers

4 baby fennel bulbs

1 large eggplant

2 large zucchini

1 red onion

1 recipe Herb, Lemon, and Garlic
Marinade (page 235)

a few fresh herb leaves,
such as basil, dill, fennel,
mint, and parsley

extra virgin olive oil, to taste

freshly squeezed lemon juice,
to taste

sea salt and freshly ground
black pepper

bread or grilled polenta, to serve

serves 4

Cut the bell peppers into quarters and remove and discard the
seeds. Trim the fennel, reserving the fronds, and cut the bulbs
into ¼-inch slices. Cut the eggplant into thick slices and cut in
half again. Cut the zucchini into thick slices diagonally and cut
the onion into wedges.

Put all the vegetables in a large bowl, add the marinade, and toss
gently until evenly coated. Cover and let marinate in a cool place
for at least 1 hour.

Preheat the grill, then cook the vegetables on the grill rack
until they are tender and lightly charred. Let cool, then peel the
bell peppers.

Arrange the vegetables on a large platter, sprinkle with the herbs,
reserved fennel fronds, olive oil, and lemon juice, then season
lightly with salt and pepper.

Serve at room temperature with crusty bread or grilled polenta.

The nut sauce, tarator, served with these leeks is found in Middle Eastern cooking, though cooks there would use ground almonds or walnuts. If the sauce is made in advance, beat it well before use.

charred leeks with tarator sauce

1½ lb. baby leeks, trimmed

2–3 tablespoons extra virgin olive oil

sea salt

a few lemon wedges, to serve

tarator sauce

2 oz. macadamia nuts, toasted

1 oz. fresh bread crumbs, ½ cup

2 garlic cloves, crushed

½ cup extra virgin olive oil

1 tablespoon freshly squeezed lemon juice

sea salt and freshly ground black pepper

serves 4

To make the sauce, put the nuts in a food processor and grind coarsely, then add the bread crumbs, garlic, and salt and pepper, and process again to form a smooth paste. Transfer to a bowl and very gradually beat in the olive oil, lemon juice, and 2 tablespoons boiling water to form a sauce. Season to taste with salt and pepper.

Preheat the grill. Brush the leeks with a little olive oil, season with salt, and cook over medium-hot coals for 6 to 10 minutes, turning occasionally, until charred and tender. Transfer to a plate, sprinkle with olive oil, then pour the sauce over the top. Serve with lemon wedges.

*14 oz. canned corn
kernels, drained*

½ cup polenta

⅓ cup all-purpose flour

1 teaspoon baking powder

½ teaspoon baking soda

½ teaspoon salt

⅔ cup buttermilk

1 tablespoon vegetable oil

½ extra large egg

olive oil, for spraying

to serve

smoked salmon

sour cream or crème fraîche

salmon caviar

serves 4

To cook these delicious cakes, you will need a grill with a flat plate. Alternatively, you can use a flat griddle or skillet preheated over the hot coals. Either way, they taste absolutely wonderful.

corn cakes

Put half the corn in a food processor and blend until fairly smooth. Add the polenta, flour, baking powder, baking soda, salt, buttermilk, vegetable oil, and egg and blend to form a thick batter. Transfer to a bowl and stir in the remaining corn kernels.

Preheat the flat plate on your grill to low and spray with olive oil. Spoon on the batter to make 4 cakes, 4 inches in diameter, and cook for 2 minutes. Using a spatula, flip and cook for a further 30 seconds, or until golden on both sides and firm to the touch. If you don't have a flat plate, use a heavy griddle or skillet, either on the barbecue, or on the stove. Transfer to a plate and keep the corn cakes warm.

Repeat to make 8 cakes. Serve, topped with smoked salmon, sour cream or crème fraîche, and salmon caviar.

Coating the shrimp with sea salt protects the
flesh during cooking so when you peel them,
the meat inside is sweet and moist.

147

grilling

salt-crusted shrimp
with tomato, avocado, and olive salad

To prepare the salad, put the tomatoes and avocado on a plate with the olives and mint. Put the olive oil and vinegar in a bowl and stir well, then sprinkle over the salad. Sprinkle the Parmesan shavings over the top and season with salt and pepper to taste.

Using kitchen shears, cut down the back of each shrimp to reveal the intestinal vein. Pull it out and discard, but leave the shell on. Wash the shrimp under cold running water, pat dry with paper towels, and put in a bowl. Sprinkle over the olive oil and toss well. Put the salt on a plate and use to coat the shrimp.

Preheat the grill, then cook the shrimp over hot coals for 2 to 3 minutes on each side, until cooked through. Let cool slightly, peel off the shells, then serve with the tomato, avocado, and olive salad.

*note To reduce balsamic vinegar, put 1¼ cups in a saucepan and boil gently until it has reduced by about two-thirds and it has reached the consistency of thick syrup. Let cool, then store in a clean jar or bottle.

20 large uncooked shell-on shrimp

1 tablespoon extra virgin olive oil

3 tablespoons sea salt

tomato, avocado, and olive salad

4–6 large ripe tomatoes, sliced

1 large ripe avocado, cut in half, pitted, and sliced

2 oz. black olives, such as Niçoise, pitted

a handful of fresh mint leaves

¼ cup extra virgin olive oil

1 tablespoon reduced balsamic vinegar*

shavings of fresh Parmesan cheese

sea salt and freshly ground black pepper

serves 4

Sea scallops grilled on the half shell look just great. If you can't find any scallop shells, don't despair, simply thread whole scallops onto soaked wooden skewers, brush with the melted butter mixture, and grill for 1 minute on each side. Serve, sprinkled with the remaining butter and cilantro.

scallops with lemongrass and lime butter

2 stalks of lemongrass

grated zest and juice of
½ large unwaxed lime

1 stick butter, softened

1 fresh red bird's eye chile,
seeded and finely chopped

1 tablespoon Thai fish sauce

24 large sea scallops

24 scallop shells

1 tablespoon chopped
fresh cilantro

freshly ground black pepper

serves 4

Using a sharp knife, trim the lemongrass stalks to about 6 inches, then remove and discard the tough outer leaves. Chop the inner stalk very thinly and put in a saucepan with the lime zest and juice, butter, chile, and fish sauce. Heat gently until the butter has melted, then simmer for 1 minute. Remove the pan from the heat and let cool.

Put the scallops on the shells and spoon a little of the butter mixture over each one.

Preheat the grill, then put the shells on the grill rack and cook for 3 to 4 minutes, turning the scallops over halfway through with tongs. Serve at once, sprinkled with chopped cilantro and freshly ground black pepper.

This is a great way to cook clams on the grill, where all the wonderful juices are collected in the foil package. Mop them up with plenty of crusty bread.

clam packages with garlic butter

2 lb. littleneck clams

1¼ sticks unsalted butter, softened

grated zest and juice of ½ unwaxed lemon

2 garlic cloves, chopped

2 tablespoons chopped fresh parsley

freshly ground black pepper

crusty bread, to serve

serves 4

Wash the clams under cold running water and scrub the shells. Discard any with broken shells or any that don't close when tapped lightly with a knife. Shake them dry and divide between 4 pieces of foil.

Put the butter, lemon zest and juice, garlic, parsley, and pepper in a bowl and beat well, then divide equally between the 4 piles of clams. Wrap the foil over the clams and seal the edges to form packages.

Preheat the grill, then put the packages on the grill rack and cook for 5 minutes. Check 1 package to see if the clams have opened and serve if ready, or cook a little longer, if needed. Serve with crusty bread.

A great way to prepare whole salmon is to remove the central bone from the fish, then tie the two fillets back together. If your filleting skills are limited, just ask your fish seller to fillet the whole fish for you.

whole salmon stuffed with herbs

Put the salmon fillets flat on a board, flesh side up. Carefully pull out any remaining bones with tweezers.

Put the butter, herbs, lemon zest, garlic, and plenty of pepper in a small bowl and beat well. Spread the mixture over one of the salmon fillets and put the second on the top, arranging them top to tail.

Using kitchen twine, tie the fish together at 1-inch intervals. Brush with a little oil, sprinkle with salt and pepper, and cook on the flat plate of an outdoor grill for 10 minutes on each side. Let rest for a further 10 minutes. Remove the twine and serve the fish cut into portions.

4 lb. whole salmon, filleted

1 stick butter, softened

1 cup chopped, fresh soft-leaf mixed herbs, such as basil, chives, mint, parsley, and tarragon

grated zest of 1 unwaxed lemon

1 garlic clove, crushed

sea salt and freshly ground black pepper

olive oil, for brushing

serves 8

This is a typical Greek dish of char-grilled bream with oil, oregano, and garlic. If you can't find bream, use other small fish such as snapper, or even trout.

grilled fish
bathed in oregano and lemon

2 lemons

1 cup extra virgin olive oil

1 tablespoon dried oregano

2 garlic cloves, finely chopped

2 tablespoons chopped fresh flat-leaf parsley

6 bream or snapper, about 12 oz. each, well cleaned and scaled

sea salt and freshly ground black pepper

serves 6

Grate the zest of 1 lemon into a small bowl and squeeze in the juice. Add ¾ cup of the oil, the oregano, garlic, parsley, salt, and pepper. Cover and steep for at least 1 hour.

Wash and dry the fish inside and out. Using a sharp knife, cut several slashes into each side. Squeeze the juice from the remaining lemon into a bowl, add the remaining ¼ cup of oil, salt, and pepper, and rub the mixture all over the fish.

Heat the flat plate of an outdoor grill for 10 minutes, add the fish, and cook for 3 to 4 minutes on each side, until charred and cooked through. Alternatively, use a large, heavy skillet or stove-top grill pan. Transfer to a large, warm platter, pour the dressing over it, and let rest for 5 minutes before serving.

Panini, which is Italian for "toasted sandwiches," can be assembled in advance, then cooked just before you want to serve them. The combination of grilled peppers, tender chicken, and a delicious arugula aïoli is definitely hard to beat.

chicken panini with roasted pepper and arugula aïoli

Preheat the grill, then cook the bell peppers over hot coals or under a preheated broiler for about 20 minutes, until charred all over. Put in a plastic bag and let cool. Peel, discard the seeds, then cut the flesh into strips.

To make the aïoli, put the egg yolk, vinegar, and a little salt and pepper in a food processor and blend briefly until frothy. Add the arugula and garlic and pulse for 30 seconds. With the machine still running, gradually pour in the olive oil through the feed tube, until the sauce is thickened and speckled vividly green. Taste and add more salt and pepper, if necessary.

Spread a little of the arugula aïoli onto the cut sides of each roll and fill the rolls with the chicken, bell pepper strips, and spinach leaves. Press the halves together.

Preheat the flat plate on the grill and cook the panini over low heat for 4 to 5 minutes on each side, until toasted. If you don't have a flat plate, cook on a cast-iron griddle. Serve hot.

2 red bell peppers, left whole

4 small focaccia or Turkish rolls, cut in half

2 large, cooked chicken breast portions, shredded into long pieces

a small handful of baby spinach

arugula aïoli

1 egg yolk

1 teaspoon white wine vinegar

a bunch of arugula, about 2 oz., coarsely chopped

1 garlic clove, crushed

⅔ cup olive oil

sea salt and freshly ground black pepper

serves 4

Jerk seasoning is Jamaica's popular spice mix, used to spark up meat, poultry, and fish, especially the delicious grilled offerings sold at the roadside jerk huts. The seasoning is a combination of allspice, cinnamon, chile, nutmeg, thyme, and sugar and is available in powder or paste form from larger supermarkets and specialty food stores.*

12 chicken wings

2 tablespoons extra virgin olive oil

1 tablespoon jerk seasoning powder* or 2 tablespoons paste

freshly squeezed juice of ½ lemon

1 teaspoon sea salt

avocado salsa

1 large ripe avocado

2 ripe tomatoes, peeled, seeded, and chopped

1 garlic clove, crushed

1 small red chile, seeded and chopped

freshly squeezed juice of ½ lemon

2 tablespoons chopped fresh cilantro

1 tablespoon extra virgin olive oil

sea salt and freshly ground black pepper

serves 4

jerk chicken wings with avocado salsa

Put the chicken wings in a ceramic dish. Mix the oil, jerk seasoning, lemon juice, and salt in a bowl, pour it over the wings, and stir well to coat. Cover and let marinate overnight in the refrigerator.

The next day cook the wings either on a preheated outdoor grill or under a hot broiler for 5 to 6 minutes on each side, basting occasionally with any remaining marinade until charred and tender.

Meanwhile, to make the salsa, put all the ingredients in a bowl, mix well, and season to taste with salt and pepper. Serve the wings with the salsa.

*note If you don't have any jerk seasoning on hand, try another spice mix or spice paste instead. Just remember, jerk is very fiery indeed, so you need a spicy one.

chicken skewers
with thyme and sesame

This spice dip, called *zahtar*, is served with pita bread. It's a mild, fragrant mixture of fresh thyme and toasted sesame seeds–very easy to make.

3 tablespoons extra virgin olive oil

1½ lb. boneless chicken breast portions

zahtar spice mix

3 tablespoons sesame seeds, toasted

½ cup fresh thyme leaves

½ teaspoon sea salt

to serve

chile oil

freshly squeezed juice of 1–2 lemons

mixed salad greens

8 wooden skewers soaked in cold water for 30 minutes

serves 4

To make the zahtar spice mix, toast the sesame seeds in a dry skillet over medium heat, until golden and aromatic. Remove from the skillet, let cool on a plate, then transfer to a spice grinder (or clean coffee grinder). Add the thyme and salt, then blend to a coarse powder. Alternatively, use a mortar and pestle. You will need 3 tablespoons for this recipe (put the remainder in an airtight container and keep in a cool place for future use).

Put the 3 tablespoons zahtar spice mix and olive oil in a shallow dish and mix well. Cut the chicken into bite-size pieces, add to the zahtar oil, and toss well until coated. Cover and let marinate in the refrigerator for at least 2 hours.

Preheat the grill, then thread the chicken pieces onto the soaked wooden skewers and cook over hot coals for 2 to 3 minutes on each side. Remove from the heat, let rest briefly, sprinkle with chile oil and lemon juice, and serve hot with salad greens.

grilled mexican-style cornish hens

Preheat a broiler until hot. Add the corn and cook for about 15 minutes, turning frequently, until charred on all sides. Let cool. Next, broil the chile peppers, until the skins are charred all over. Transfer to a bowl and let cool.

Using a sharp knife, cut down all sides of the corn cob to remove the kernels. Put them in a bowl. Peel and seed the chile peppers, chop the flesh, then add to the corn. Stir in all the remaining salsa ingredients, season to taste with salt and pepper. Set aside.

To butterfly the hens, turn them breast side down and, using poultry shears or sturdy kitchen shears, cut down each side of the backbone and discard it. Turn the birds over and open them out flat, pressing down hard on the breastbone. Thread 2 skewers diagonally through each hen from the wings to the thigh bones.

To make the marinade, skewer the chile peppers and garlic together and cook under a preheated medium-hot broiler for 10 minutes, turning frequently, until evenly browned. Scrape off and discard the skins from the chile peppers and chop the flesh coarsely. Put the flesh and seeds in a blender, add the garlic and all the remaining marinade ingredients, and blend to a purée.

Pour the marinade over the hens and let marinate in the refrigerator overnight. Return them to room temperature for 1 hour before cooking, then remove the birds from their marinade, and grill over medium-hot coals for 12 minutes on each side, basting occasionally. Let rest for 5 minutes. Serve with the corn salsa.

4 Cornish game hens

mexican marinade

4 jalapeño chile peppers

8 garlic cloves, peeled

¼ cup freshly squeezed orange juice

2 tablespoons freshly squeezed lime juice

1 tablespoon ground cumin

1 tablespoon dried oregano or thyme

2 teaspoons sea salt

⅓ cup olive oil

1 tablespoon maple syrup or honey

creamy corn salsa

1 ear of fresh corn, husk removed

2 red chile peppers, such as serrano

1 tomato, diced

1 garlic clove, crushed

freshly squeezed juice of ½ lime

1 tablespoon maple syrup

2 tablespoons sour cream

sea salt and freshly ground black pepper

8 metal skewers

serves 4

lamb burgers
with mint yogurt

A good burger should be thick, moist, tender, and juicy. These lamb burgers are all that and more. Serve in crusty rolls with a few slices of tomato, plenty of fresh salad greens, and a generous spoonful of the cool minty yogurt dressing. The perfect burger for a patio picnic.

Put the lamb and pork in a food processor and process briefly until coarsely ground. Transfer to a bowl and, using your hands, work in the chopped onion, garlic, cumin, cinnamon, oregano, salt, bread crumbs, capers, pepper, and beaten egg. Cover and let marinate in the refrigerator for at least 2 hours.

Put the yogurt and cream in a bowl, stir in the mint, with salt and pepper to taste.

Using damp hands, shape the meat into 8 burgers. Preheat the grill, then brush the grill rack with oil. Cook the burgers for about 3 minutes on each side.

Split the rolls in half and fill with the cooked burgers, salad greens, tomato slices, and a spoonful of mint yogurt. Serve immediately.

variation For a traditional hamburger, replace the lamb with beef, omit the spices, and instead of the capers, add 4 chopped anchovy fillets. Serve in round rolls with salad.

1½ lb. boneless lamb shoulder, cut into ½-inch cubes

4 oz. salt pork, chopped

1 onion, very finely chopped

2 garlic cloves, crushed

2 tablespoon ground cumin

2 teaspoons ground cinnamon

1 tablespoon dried oregano

2 teaspoons sea salt

½ cup fresh bread crumbs

1 tablespoon capers, drained and chopped

1 extra large egg, beaten

freshly ground black pepper

mint yogurt

1 cup plain yogurt

2 tablespoons heavy cream

2 tablespoons chopped fresh mint leaves

sea salt and freshly ground black pepper

to serve

4 crusty rolls

salad greens

tomato slices

serves 4

lamb kabobs
with warm chickpea salad

1½ lb. lamb tenderloin

1 recipe Minted Yogurt Marinade
(page 235)

warm chickpea salad

1 cup dried chickpeas, soaked
overnight in cold water, drained
and rinsed

1 bay leaf

½ onion

⅓ cup extra virgin olive oil, plus
extra to serve

1 garlic clove, finely chopped

freshly squeezed juice
of ½ lemon

a handful of fresh parsley

a pinch of sweet paprika

sea salt and freshly ground
black pepper

4 metal skewers

serves 4

Pieces of tender lamb, marinated in mint and yogurt, complement the warm chickpeas perfectly. Serve this as part of a splendid Middle Eastern feast with Hummus (page 179) and Flatbreads (page 184).

Using a sharp knife, cut the lamb into bite-size pieces and put in a shallow dish. Add the marinade and stir well to coat the lamb. Let marinate in the refrigerator for 2 to 4 hours. Thread onto the skewers.

Prepare the chickpea salad about 1 hour before cooking the lamb. Put the soaked chickpeas, bay leaf, and onion in a heavy saucepan and cover with cold water. Bring to a boil and simmer for 45 minutes or until the chickpeas are tender, skimming off the foam from time to time.

Drain the chickpeas and transfer to a bowl. Remove and discard the onion and bay leaf. Mash coarsely with a fork. Stir in the olive oil, garlic, lemon juice, parsley, paprika, and salt and pepper to taste.

Meanwhile, preheat the grill, then cook the kabobs over hot coals for 6 to 8 minutes, turning halfway through, until tender. Serve the kabobs on a bed of chickpea salad, sprinkled with a little extra olive oil.

2 racks barbecue spareribs,
1 lb. each

chile-spiked cornbread

1¼ cups medium cornmeal

1¼ cups all-purpose flour

1½ teaspoons salt

1 tablespoon baking powder

2 eggs, beaten

1 cup milk

2 tablespoons olive oil

2 large red chile peppers, such as
Anaheim or New Mexico, seeded
and chopped

1 cup canned corn kernels,
drained

¼ cup finely grated
Cheddar cheese

2 tablespoons chopped
fresh cilantro

sweet chile marinade

2 garlic cloves, crushed

2 tablespoons sea salt

2 tablespoons ground cumin

2 teaspoons chilli powder

1 teaspoon dried oregano

½ cup maple syrup or honey

¼ cup red wine vinegar

¼ cup olive oil

a cake pan, 8 inches square,
greased and base-lined with
parchment paper

serves 4–6

Nibbling away at succulent pork ribs is one of the true pleasures of an outdoor grill—(providing of course you eat meat). Here they are cooked in a marinade of spices and maple syrup giving them the authentic flavor of the Deep South.

tex-mex pork rack

To make the cornbread, put the cornmeal, flour, salt, and baking powder in a bowl and mix. Make a well in the center and pour in the eggs, milk, and olive oil. Beat with a wooden spoon to make a smooth batter. Fold in the chile peppers, corn, cheese, and cilantro, then spoon into the prepared cake pan. Bake in a preheated oven at 400°F for 25 minutes, or until a skewer inserted in the center comes out clean.

Remove from the oven and let cool in the pan for about 5 minutes, then invert onto a wire rack to cool completely.

Wash the ribs and pat them dry with paper towels. Transfer to a shallow, non-metal dish. Put all the marinade ingredients in a bowl, mix well, pour over the ribs, then work in well with your hands. Cover and let marinate overnight in the refrigerator.

The next day, return the ribs to room temperature for 1 hour, then cook on a preheated medium-hot outdoor grill for about 30 minutes, turning and basting frequently with the juices. Let cool a little, then serve with the cornbread.

Don't overcook pork or it will be dry and tough. A good
test is to pierce the meat with a skewer, leave it there
for a second, remove it, and carefully feel how hot it is—
it should feel warm, not too hot or too cold.

sage-rubbed pork chops

2 tablespoons chopped
fresh sage leaves

2 tablespoons
whole-grain mustard

2 tablespoons extra virgin
olive oil

4 large pork chops

sea salt and freshly ground
black pepper

smoky tomato salsa

4 ripe plum tomatoes

2 hot fresh red chiles,
about 2 inches long,
seeded and chopped

4 garlic cloves, peeled

1 red onion, cut into wedges

¼ cup extra virgin olive oil

1 tablespoon freshly
squeezed lemon juice

2 tablespoons chopped
fresh cilantro

sea salt and freshly ground
black pepper

2 wooden skewers, soaked in
cold water for 30 minutes

serves 4

Put the sage, mustard, and olive oil in a bowl and mix well.
Season with a little salt and pepper, then spread the
mixture all over the chops. Let marinate in the refrigerator
for 1 hour.

Meanwhile, preheat the grill. To make the salsa, hold the
tomatoes over the flames of the grill with tongs for about
1 minute, turning frequently, until the skin is charred all
over. Let cool, peel, cut in half, and remove and discard
the seeds. Chop the flesh. Repeat with the chiles.

Thread the garlic cloves and onion quarters onto separate
skewers. Cook the garlic over hot coals for 3 to 4 minutes
and the onion for 10 to 12 minutes, turning frequently, until
they are charred and softened. Let cool, remove from the
skewers, and cut into cubes.

Put the tomatoes, chiles, garlic, and onion in a bowl and
stir in the olive oil, lemon juice, and cilantro. Season to
taste with salt and pepper.

Cook the chops over hot coals for 2½ to 3 minutes on
each side, until browned and cooked through. Serve hot
with the smoky tomato salsa.

Choosing the right cut for grilling is the first step to producing the perfect steak. There are several you can use, such as New York strip steak, T-bone, or sirloin, but this recipe suggests Delmonico steak. This is the "eye" of the rib roast and is marbled with fat, giving a moist result. It has a good flavor and is not too huge.

delmonico steak with anchovy butter

Put the butter, anchovies, parsley, and a little pepper in a bowl and beat well. Transfer to a sheet of foil and roll up into a log. Chill until needed.

Preheat the grill to high and brush the grill rack with oil. Season the steaks with salt and pepper and cook for 3 minutes on each side for rare, 4 to 5 minutes for medium, and 5 to 6 minutes for well done.

Transfer the steaks to a warmed serving plate and top each one with 2 slices of the anchovy butter. Let rest for about 5 minutes before serving in order to set the juices.

1¼ sticks butter, softened

8 anchovy fillets in oil, drained and coarsely chopped

2 tablespoons chopped fresh parsley

4 Delmonico steaks, about 8 oz. each

oil, for brushing

sea salt and freshly ground black pepper

serves 4

dips & breads

2 cups dried peeled fava beans

1 fresh bouquet garni of parsley, celery, bay leaf, and thyme

1 large onion, chopped

1 potato, unpeeled

4 garlic cloves, chopped

¼ cup extra virgin olive oil, plus extra to serve (optional)

freshly squeezed juice of 1 lemon (4–5 tablespoons)

6 sprigs of oregano, chopped, plus extra to serve

sea salt and freshly ground black pepper

to serve

your choice of:
baby leafy vegetables
radishes
cucumber
crusty bread, toasted

serves 4

All around the Mediterranean, fresh and dried peas, beans, and lentils are used in dips and spreads, as sauces with pasta, and in soups. Depending on the region and local herbs, different flavors and ingredients are used. The constant is dried fava beans, known as faba beans. The best are the skinless type: they cook quickly, taste better, and have a more delicate texture.

italian bean dip

Soak the beans for 4 hours or overnight in cold water, or cheat by putting them in a saucepan, covering them with boiling water, bringing to a boil, and soaking for 2 hours with the heat turned off. Drain, then put them in a large saucepan with the bunch of herbs, onion, and potato and add 2 quarts boiling water. Bring to a boil, boil hard for 10 minutes, reduce the heat, and cook, partially covered, for 1½ to 2 hours, or until you can crush the beans easily with your thumbnail.

Drain the vegetables, reserving 2 to 3 tablespoons of liquid. Discard the herbs. Working in batches if necessary, put the beans, potato, onion, and garlic in a food processor, with the olive oil, lemon juice, oregano, salt, and pepper. Blend in short bursts to a grainy but creamy purée.

Serve hot (as a side dish), warm, or cool, sprinkled with extra olive oil and a few oregano leaves. Serve as a dip or spread with baby leafy vegetables, radishes, and cucumber or with bread chunks, or a combination.

Yogurt in Greece is so rich, sharp, and solid that it's almost like cheese, not yogurt. If you can't find the real thing, you can strain plain yogurt through cheesecloth set in a strainer. You could also mix in cream cheese or even mash in a little feta cheese for stiffness. The finished dish should hold its shape. A dribble of greeny-gold, Greek oil over the top is the final, and essential, detail.

tzatziki

8 oz. cucumber, unpeeled

2 teaspoons salt

3 garlic cloves, crushed

1½ cups strained plain yogurt, preferably Greek-style

¼ cup extra virgin olive oil

to serve (optional)

fresh mint or parsley, chopped

black olives

bread

cucumber, cut in strips

carrots, cut in strips

serves 4–6, makes about 3 cups

Grate the cucumber coarsely, put it in a non-metal bowl, sprinkle with the salt, stir, and let stand for 10 minutes. Put in a non-metal strainer and press hard to squeeze out the salt and liquid. Do not rinse. Return to a clean bowl and stir in the garlic and yogurt.

Spoon into small individual serving dishes and drizzle with a little olive oil. Serve with chopped herbs, black olives, bread, cucumber, and carrots.

Lemony, fresh hummus, and *hummus bi tahini* (containing toasted sesame seed paste) are delicious Middle Eastern snack foods. The sesame richness has a more intense effect: but the simpler chickpea purée is also good. If possible, find dried chickpeas without skins (Greek grocers sometimes stock them). For 10-minute hummus use canned chickpeas.

hummus

If using dried chickpeas, put them in a bowl, cover with boiling water, and let soak for 3 hours (or in cold water for 8 hours). Drain. Put in a large saucepan, cover with boiling water, bring to a boil, partially cover, and simmer for 1½ to 2½ hours, or until the chickpeas are easily crushable and tender. Drain.

Put the chickpeas in a food processor with the lemon juice, garlic, ¼ teaspoon salt, pepper, and the tahini paste, if using. Blend briefly to a mousse. With the machine running, drizzle the oil through the feed tube to form a creamy purée. Season to taste with salt and pepper.

Serve cool or chilled. You can also sprinkle a little hot red paprika on top and add the traditional trickle of extra virgin olive oil. Serve with crisp lettuce leaves and other crisp raw vegetables, and heated, torn flatbreads.

1 cup dried chickpeas or 2 cups cooked

freshly squeezed juice of 1 lemon

2 garlic cloves, crushed

2 tablespoons tahini paste (optional)

½ cup extra virgin olive oil

sea salt and freshly ground black pepper

to serve

hot paprika

extra virgin olive oil

lettuce leaves

crisp raw vegetables

flatbreads

serves 6–8: makes about 2 cups

Beet hummus is a delicious summery dip for vegetables or toasted bread. Cooking bread on the grill or a ridged stove-top grill pan is easy and very like the traditional way that pita bread is cooked.

beet hummus

with pan-grilled bread

8 oz. cooked beets in natural juices, drained and chopped

½ cup white bread crumbs

1 garlic clove, crushed

3 tablespoons extra virgin olive oil

2 tablespoons grated horseradish

1 tablespoon freshly squeezed lemon juice

sea salt and freshly ground black pepper

bread

2¼ cups white bread flour, plus extra for kneading

1 teaspoon sea salt

1 teaspoon active dry yeast

1 tablespoon olive oil, plus extra for oiling the bowl

serves 6

To make the bread dough, sift the flour into the bowl of an electric mixer* with the dough hook attached. Stir in the salt and yeast, then gradually work in ⅓ cup warm water and the oil to make a soft dough. Transfer to a lightly floured surface and knead for 8 to 10 minutes, until smooth and elastic.

Put the dough in an oiled bowl, cover with plastic wrap, and let rise in a warm place for 45 minutes, or until doubled in size.

Meanwhile, to make the hummus, put the beets, bread crumbs, garlic, oil, horseradish, and lemon juice in a food processor, blend to a smooth purée, and season with salt and pepper to taste.

Transfer the dough to a lightly floured surface and knead it gently. Divide into 6 pieces and roll out each one to an oval, about the size of a pita bread. Cook the bread over medium-hot coals or on a ridged stove-top grill pan for 1 to 2 minutes on each side. Serve warm with the hummus.

*note If you don't have an electric mixer, use a food processor with the plastic blade attachment.

focaccia
with olives

This dough is a quick food-processor version, which was originally developed for pizzas, but it makes excellent focaccia too. You could vary the recipe by using lemon instead of orange, and dried or fresh oregano instead of rosemary, plus other toppings such as anchovy-stuffed green olives.

1 package active dry yeast,
2 ¼ teaspoons

2 cups all-purpose flour, plus
¼ cup for shaping

½ teaspoon sea salt flakes

2 tablespoons extra virgin
olive oil, preferably Italian

topping

zest of 1 orange, finely
shredded, using a zester

grated zest and juice of
1 unwaxed orange

¼ cup extra virgin olive oil

2 garlic cloves, crushed

2 tablespoons fresh rosemary
leaves, coarsely chopped

½ teaspoon coarsely
crushed black pepper

1 teaspoon sea salt
flakes or crystals

1 cup dry-cured black olives

a baking tray, oiled

serves 4

Put the yeast, flour, and sea salt in a food processor fitted with a plastic blade. Pulse briefly to sift the ingredients. Combine the oil with ⅔ cup warm water and, with the machine running, pour it all through the feed tube. Process, in short bursts, for 15 seconds, until a soft mass forms (not a ball). It will be sticky and soft.

Scoop out the dough adding the extra ¼ cup flour as you knead, roll, pat, and thump down the dough for 2 minutes on a counter. Put the ball of dough in an oiled bowl. Enclose the whole bowl in a large plastic bag. Leave in a warm place until the dough has doubled in size, about 50 minutes.

Pat and stretch the dough into a rectangle 10 x 8 inches. Transfer to an oiled baking tray. Prod the dough all over with your fingertips to form dimples to take the topping.

Mix the orange zest and juice, oil, garlic, rosemary, pepper, and half the salt in a bowl. Pour the mixture over the dough. Sprinkle with the olives, pushing them into the dimples. Let rest for 30 minutes.

Bake in a preheated oven at 400°F for 25 to 30 minutes, or until crusty and aromatic. Sprinkle with the remaining salt. Cut into generous squares, then serve hot or warm.

Hot from the grill, this aromatic herb bread is delicious used to mop up the wonderful meat juices from a grill party, or eaten on its own with olive oil for dipping.

grilled rosemary flatbread

1²/₃ cups white bread flour, plus extra for dusting

1½ teaspoons active dry yeast

1 teaspoon salt

1 tablespoon chopped fresh rosemary

½ cup hand-hot water

2 tablespoons extra virgin olive oil, plus extra for brushing

serves 4

Sift the flour into the bowl of a stand-up mixer and stir in the yeast, salt, and rosemary. Add the hot water and olive oil and knead with the dough hook at high speed for about 8 minutes, or until the dough is smooth and elastic. Alternatively, sift the flour into a large bowl and stir in the yeast, salt, and rosemary. Make a well in the center, then add the hot water and olive oil and mix to form a soft dough. Turn out onto a lightly floured counter and knead until the dough is smooth and elastic.

Shape the dough into a ball, then put in an oiled bowl, cover with a dish towel and let rise in a warm place for 45 to 60 minutes or until doubled in size.

Punch down the dough and divide into fourths. Roll each piece out on a lightly floured counter to make a 6-inch long oval.

Preheat the grill to low or wait until the coals are giving off a low heat. Brush the bread with a little olive oil and cook for 5 minutes, then brush the top with the remaining olive oil, flip, and cook for 4 to 5 minutes more, until the bread is cooked through. Serve hot.

sweet things
& drinks

grilled figs
with almond mascarpone cream

¾ cup mascarpone cheese

½ teaspoon vanilla extract

1 tablespoon toasted
ground almonds, or slivered
almonds crushed to
a powder with a mortar
and pestle

1 tablespoon Marsala wine

1 tablespoon honey

1 tablespoon sugar

1 teaspoon ground
cardamom

8–10 figs, cut in half

serves 4

This dish works well with pitted fruits too, such as plums, peaches, or nectarines.

Put the mascarpone cheese, vanilla, almonds, Marsala, and honey in a bowl and beat well. Cover and chill until needed.

Mix the sugar and ground cardamom in another bowl, then carefully dip the cut surface of the figs in the mixture.

Preheat the grill, then cook the figs over medium-hot coals for 1 to 2 minutes on each side, until charred and softened.

Transfer the grilled figs to 4 serving bowls and serve with the almond mascarpone cream.

Wrapping fruits in foil is a great way to cook them on the grill—all the juices are contained in the package while the fruit softens.

grilled fruit packages

4 peaches or nectarines, cut in half, pitted, and sliced

2 cups blueberries

⅔ cup raspberries

freshly squeezed juice of 1 orange

1 teaspoon ground cinnamon

2 tablespoons sugar

1 cup yogurt

2 tablespoons heavy cream

1 tablespoon honey

1 tablespoon rose water

1 tablespoon chopped pistachios

serves 4

Put the fruit in a large bowl, add the orange juice, cinnamon, and sugar, and mix well. Divide the fruit mixture among 4 sheets of foil. Fold the foil over the fruit and seal the edges to make packages.

Mix the yogurt, cream, honey, and rose water in another bowl. Chill until needed.

Preheat the grill, then cook the packages over medium-hot coals for 5 to 6 minutes. Remove the packages from the heat, open carefully, and transfer to 4 serving bowls. Serve with the yogurt and a sprinkling of pistachios.

toasted coconut ice cream
with grilled pineapple

*1 pineapple, medium
or small, with leafy top
if possible, cut lengthwise into
wedges and core removed*

½ cup brown sugar

1 stick unsalted butter

⅓ cup dark rum

ice cream

*⅓ cup dried unsweetened
shredded coconut*

1¾ cups heavy cream

1¼ cups coconut milk

½ cup sugar

5 egg yolks

an ice cream maker (optional)

serves 6

To make the ice cream, put the coconut in a dry skillet and toast, stirring over medium heat for 2 to 3 minutes, until evenly browned. Transfer to a saucepan, then add the cream, coconut milk, and sugar. Heat gently until it just reaches boiling point.

Put the egg yolks in a bowl and beat with a wooden spoon until pale. Stir in about 2 tablespoons of the hot custard, then return the mixture to the pan. Heat gently, stirring constantly, until the mixture thickens enough to coat the back of the wooden spoon. Remove the pan from the heat and let cool completely.

When cold, strain the custard, and freeze in an ice cream maker according to the manufacturer's instructions. Transfer to the freezer until required. Alternatively, pour the cold custard into a plastic container and freeze for 5 hours, beating at hourly intervals with a balloon whisk.

Put the sugar, butter, and rum in a small saucepan and heat until the sugar dissolves. Brush a little of the mixture over the pineapple wedges, then cook them on a preheated outdoor grill or on a stove-top grill pan for 2 minutes on each side until charred and tender. Remove from the heat and, holding the flesh with a fork, cut between the skin and flesh with a sharp knife. Cut the flesh into segments to make it easier to eat, then reassemble the wedges. Serve with the ice cream and remaining rum sauce, about 2 tablespoons each.

No one can resist perfect crumbling crust piled with mixed fruits and served with softly whipped cream. With this quantity of dough, it's easier to make it in two batches.

blue and red berry tarts

pastry dough

4¾ cups all-purpose flour, plus extra for dusting

¾ cup sugar

4¾ sticks butter

6 egg yolks

filling

2¼ cups blueberries

2½ cups confectioners' sugar, plus extra for dusting

6 cups heavy cream

2 lb. strawberries, hulled and cut into bite-size pieces

1 lb. raspberries, about 2⅔ cups

2¼ cups blackberries

3 loose-based tart pans, 9 inches diameter, buttered

wax paper and baking beans or uncooked rice

serves 20

Put half the flour, half the sugar, and half the butter in a food processor and blend until the mixture looks like bread crumbs. Add 3 of the egg yolks and process again until the mixture forms a ball. Remove and repeat with the remaining dough ingredients. Combine, then divide into 3 equal amounts. Wrap separately in plastic wrap and chill for about 20 minutes.

Transfer to a lightly floured counter and roll out each dough portion until just larger than the tart pans. Line each pan with dough, prick the base with a fork, and chill for 20 minutes.

Line the chilled pie shells with wax paper and baking beans or rice. Cook in a preheated oven at 350°F for 20 minutes. Remove the baking beans and paper, reduce to 325°F, and cook for a further 20 minutes until dry and golden.

Put the blueberries and 1¼ cups confectioners' sugar in a small saucepan. Add ½ cup water and simmer gently for 5 minutes, until the berries are soft. Remove from the heat and let cool.

Put the cream in a bowl, add the remaining confectioners' sugar, and whip until soft peaks form. Add the strawberries, mix briefly, then spoon into the cooled pie shells. Pile the raspberries and blackberries on top. Spoon over the stewed blueberries and remove the tarts from the pans. Serve dusted with confectioners' sugar.

Vanilla syrup transforms this cake into a lovely dessert, but you can also serve it simply with a spoonful of yogurt.

lemon cake with vanilla syrup and strawberries

1 stick unsalted butter, softened
1 cup sugar
2 lemons
2 eggs, lightly beaten
1¾ cups all-purpose flour
2 teaspoons baking powder
⅓ cup fine semolina
½ cup full-fat plain yogurt
fresh strawberries, to serve

vanilla syrup

1 vanilla bean
1 cup sugar

a springform cake pan,
9 inches diameter, greased and
base-lined with parchment

serves 6

Grate the zest and squeeze the juice from the lemons. Put the butter, sugar, and lemon zest in a bowl and beat until pale and soft. Gradually beat in the eggs, a little at a time, until evenly mixed. Fold in the flour, baking powder, and semolina, then stir in the yogurt and lemon juice.

Spoon the mixture into the prepared cake pan and bake in a preheated oven at 350°F for about 40 minutes, until risen and spongy. The cake is cooked when a toothpick inserted into the center of the cake comes out clean. Let cool in the pan for 5 minutes, then invert onto a wire rack to cool completely.

Meanwhile, to make the syrup, split the vanilla bean lengthwise with a sharp knife. Put the sugar and vanilla bean in a small saucepan and add 1¼ cups water. Heat gently until the sugar has dissolved. Bring to a boil and simmer for about 5 minutes, until it becomes syrupy. Remove from the heat and let cool a little.

To serve, cut the cake into slices while still slightly warm, pour over the syrup, and serve with strawberries.

A refreshing and summery sherbet—pretty and delicious when served with thin, crisp, almond cookies. Roasting the plums before they are puréed will intensify their flavor.

caramelized plum sherbet

*2 lb. red plums,
cut in half and pitted*

2 tablespoons sugar

*freshly squeezed juice
of ½ lemon*

*sweet almond wafer
cookies, to serve
(optional)*

sugar syrup

1¼ cups sugar

*1 vanilla bean, split
lengthwise*

*an ice cream maker
(optional)*

serves 6–8

Put the halved plums, cut side up, in an ovenproof dish, sprinkle with the sugar, and bake in a preheated oven at 400°F for 20 minutes until golden and softened. Let cool completely, then transfer to a blender, and purée until very smooth. Stir in the lemon juice.

Meanwhile, to make the sugar syrup, put the sugar and vanilla bean into a saucepan, add 2⅓ cups water, and heat gently until the sugar has dissolved. Bring to a boil, reduce the heat, and simmer for 5 minutes. Let cool, remove the vanilla bean, then stir the syrup into the plum purée.

Transfer to an ice cream maker and churn, according to the manufacturer's instructions. Store in the freezer until required.

Alternatively, transfer the purée to a plastic container and freeze for 5 hours, beating at hourly intervals with a balloon whisk. (This will break down the ice crystals and make the sherbet smooth.) Serve with the almond cookies, if using.

A wonderfully indulgent and nostalgic sundae, which is one of the most delicious of all.

knickerbocker glory

2 scoops vanilla ice cream

about 3–4 tablespoons fresh raspberries, crushed with a fork

1 scoop strawberry ice cream

1–2 tablespoons chopped fresh fruit, such as pineapple or apricots

about 1–2 tablespoons whipped cream

about 1 teaspoon toasted almonds, coarsely crushed

1 maraschino cherry

hot chocolate sauce

about 6 oz. bittersweet chocolate, broken into pieces

1 cup heavy cream, heated

¼ cup sugar

a tall soda glass

serves 1

To make the chocolate sauce, put the chocolate in a heatproof bowl and set it above a saucepan of simmering water—don't let the water touch the bowl. Remove the bowl from the heat and stir in the hot cream.

Carefully spoon about 2 tablespoons of the chocolate sauce into the bottom of a tall soda glass. Add 2 scoops vanilla ice cream, then the crushed fresh raspberries.

Add 1 scoop strawberry ice cream, then a layer of chopped fresh pineapple or apricots. Top with a big cloud of whipped cream and sprinkle with toasted almonds and a cherry.

Put a long parfait spoon into the glass and serve.

Hot sauces make a delicious contrast with cold ice cream. This one is butterscotch, but try Hot Fudge Sauce (page 204) if you prefer.

hot butterscotch sundae

To make the nut brittle, put ⅓ cup water and the sugar in a saucepan, stir, then bring to a boil over medium heat. Continue boiling until golden brown. Stir in the nuts, pour onto the prepared baking tray, then let cool and set. When set, break up the brittle, then crush with a rolling pin.

To make the butterscotch sauce, put the sugar, cream, and butter in a saucepan and stir over medium heat, until melted and boiling. Reduce the heat and simmer for 3 minutes.

Put 3 scoops chocolate or vanilla ice cream in the base of each sundae dish and balance 1 scoop coffee or vanilla ice cream on top. Spoon half the hot butterscotch sauce around the ice cream in the 4 dishes, then pour the remaining sauce over the top. Sprinkle with nut brittle and serve immediately.

12 scoops very cold chocolate or vanilla ice cream

4 scoops very cold coffee or vanilla ice cream

nut brittle

⅓ cup sugar

½ cup pecans or almonds, coarsely crushed

butterscotch sauce

½ cup brown sugar

½ cup heavy cream

⅓ cup butter

4 metal sundae dishes or thick, heatproof glass bowls

a baking tray, greased

serves 4

Fudge—whether hot or cold—is one of the great soda fountain classics. Pour hot fudge sauce over this indulgent combination of fruit and ice cream for a real summertime treat.

fudge sauce sundae

12 scoops very cold
vanilla ice cream

4 apricots, fresh or canned,
sliced (optional)

12 tablespoons stiffly
whipped cream

4 fan-shaped wafers

pineapple syrup

1 large ripe pineapple,
peeled and core removed

sugar (see method)

strawberry sauce

3 baskets strawberries

1 tablespoon freshly
squeezed lemon juice

¼ cup sugar

hot fudge sauce

4–5 oz. dark chocolate,
chopped

2 tablespoons unsalted
butter

2 tablespoons corn syrup

½ cup brown sugar

½ cup heavy cream

4 heatproof sundae glasses

serves 4

To make the pineapple syrup, cut the pineapple flesh into chunks and put in a food processor or blender. Blend until smooth, then add ½ cup sugar for every ⅔ cup pulp. Blend again. Transfer to a stainless steel saucepan, bring slowly to a boil, reduce the heat, then simmer for 10 minutes, stirring frequently. Let cool, then chill.

To make the strawberry sauce, put the strawberries, lemon juice, and sugar in a saucepan and heat gently until the juices run. When the berries have become pale and the juice dark, remove from the heat and press through a plastic strainer. Let cool.

To make the fudge sauce, put the chocolate, butter, corn syrup, sugar, and cream in a saucepan and heat, stirring, until melted. Bring to a boil, then remove from the heat.

Put 1 scoop vanilla ice cream in a sundae glass, then add 1 tablespoon pineapple syrup and 1 sliced apricot, if using. Add 3 tablespoons whipped cream, then 2 tablespoons strawberry sauce. Add 2 more scoops ice cream, then spoon 2 to 3 tablespoons hot fudge sauce over the top. Repeat to make 4 sundaes. Serve topped with a wafer.

s'mores

Here's one for the kids, and for adults who remember being kids. You can use any sweet cookie for this recipe instead of graham crackers, such as langue du chat or almond thins.

16 cookies

8 pieces of semisweet chocolate

16 marshmallows

8 metal skewers

serves 4

Put half the cookies on a large plate and top each one with a square of chocolate.

Preheat the grill. Thread 2 marshmallows onto each skewer and cook over hot coals for about 2 minutes, turning constantly until the marshmallows are melted and blackened. Remove from the heat and let cool slightly.

Put the marshmallows on top of the chocolate squares and sandwich together with the remaining cookies. Gently ease out the skewers and serve the s'mores as soon as the chocolate melts.

Whenever you squeeze fruit juice, pour some into ice cube trays and freeze for later.

fruit frappé

2 cups freshly squeezed fruit juice, such as apple, raspberry, or pineapple

serves 2

Freeze the juice in ice cube trays. When ready to serve, transfer to a food processor and process in short bursts until crushed but not slushy.

Alternatively, put the ice cubes in the refrigerator for a couple of minutes to soften a little, then mash them with a fork. Serve in chilled glasses.

Ice coffee can be surprisingly refreshing on a hot day. To make this extra special, add a tablespoon of rum or brandy.

ice coffee

½ cup strong
espresso coffee,
cooled and chilled

1 cup milk
or cream

1 scoop vanilla
ice cream

to serve

1–2 tablespoons
whipped cream

1 coffee bean,
crushed (optional)

sugar, to taste

serves 1

Put the coffee in a blender with the milk or cream and ice cream and blend until smooth. Pour into a glass and top with a swirl of whipped cream and a sprinkle of crushed coffee bean, if using. Serve sugar separately and sweeten to taste.

variation Make the ice coffee as in the main recipe, stir in 1 tablespoon rum or brandy, and top with whipped cream.

strawberry, pear, and orange frappé

1 lb. strawberries, hulled

4 pears, quartered and cored

1¼ cups freshly squeezed orange juice

ice cubes, to serve (optional)

serves 4

For this fresh juice you really need a juicer, but in a pinch you could purée the fruits in a blender. Always make fresh juices just before serving, because they discolor and separate quickly.

Push the strawberries and pears through a juicer and transfer to a pitcher. Add the orange juice, stir to mix, then pour into glasses half filled with ice cubes, if using. Serve at once.

ginger and lime cordial

A lovely refreshing cordial with a delicious kick of ginger—perfect for any occasion.

Using a sharp knife, peel and thinly slice the ginger, then pound lightly with a rolling pin. Put it in a saucepan with the lime slices and 1 quart water, bring to a boil, partially cover with a lid, and simmer gently for 45 minutes. Remove the saucepan from the heat, add the sugar, and stir until dissolved. Let cool, strain, and pour the cordial into a sterilized bottle. Seal and store until ready to use.

When ready to serve, pour a little cordial into glasses, add ice and lime wedges, and top up with sparkling water.

6 oz. fresh ginger

2 unwaxed limes, sliced

2 cups sugar

to serve

ice cubes

unwaxed lime wedges

sparkling water

1 sterilized bottle, 3 cups (page 4)

makes about 3 cups

strawberry and banana ice cream shake

2 cups ripe
strawberries, hulled

1 ripe banana, peeled
and chopped

4 scoops strawberry
ice cream, plus extra
to serve (optional)

¾ cup milk

serves 3–4

A great shake for when you're in serious ice cream mode. Also, try mango and banana with vanilla ice cream.

Put the strawberries, banana, ice cream, and milk in a blender and purée until very smooth. Pour into glasses and serve topped with extra ice cream, if using.

250 ml milk

2 teaspoons sugar or
sugar syrup*

a drop of vanilla extract

1 scoop vanilla
ice cream

125 ml crushed ice
(optional)

serves 1

* To make sugar syrup,
put 1 part sugar to
3 parts water in a
saucepan and heat
gently until the sugar
dissolves and the
mixture becomes a
light syrup.

vanilla milkshake

You can buy drink mixer machines based on the old soda fountain classics—or use a blender instead. Crushed ice will make the drink froth more.

Put all the ingredients in a blender (with the ice) or drink mixer and blend until frothy. Transfer to a metal milkshake container and serve separately with a saucer, napkins and a tall soda glass, plus straws and a parfait spoon.

variation Instead of the sugar syrup and vanilla, use 1 tablespoon Hot Chocolate Sauce (page 200).

champagne cocktails

There is something decidedly decadent about
a glass of fizz in the morning, so if you're going
to treat yourself to brunch, why not totally spoil
yourself with one of these cocktails.

campari fizz

6 shots of Campari

3 teaspoons sugar

*1 bottle chilled sparkling wine,
750 ml*

serves 6

Pour the Campari into
6 champagne flutes and add
½ teaspoon sugar to each
one. Top up with sparkling
wine and serve.

peach bellini

3 ripe peaches

*1 bottle chilled Prosecco or
sparkling wine, 750 ml*

serves 6

Peel the peaches by
plunging them into boiling
water for 30 seconds.
Refresh them under cold
water and peel off the skin.
Cut in half, remove the pit,
and chop the flesh.

Put the peaches in a blender,
add a small amount of
Prosecco, and process to a
purée. Pour into champagne
flutes and top up with the
remaining Prosecco.

mimosa

*6 blood oranges or
regular oranges*

*1 bottle chilled sparkling wine,
750 ml*

serves 6

Squeeze the oranges and
divide the juice among
6 champagne flutes. Top
up with sparkling wine
and serve.

This is a pretty spritzer to cool a hot brow on a sunny day. The frozen grapes act as original ice cubes, keeping the wine chilled and also make it look amazing.

white wine spritzer

*1 bottle white wine,
3 cups, chilled*

*4 cups sparkling mineral
water, chilled*

2 cups white grapes, frozen

serves 8

Put the chilled white wine, mineral water, and frozen grapes in a large pitcher and mix well. Serve the spritzer in your favorite large glasses.

variation Frozen fruit cubes are great for chilling picnic drinks and they don't melt as quickly as ordinary ice cubes. Try chopping up orange segments, putting them in ice cube trays, covering with a little fresh juice, then freezing them.

iced long vodka

4 shots iced vodka,
preferably Absolut

4 shots lime cordial

a few drops of
Angostura bitters

to serve

ice cubes

1 unwaxed lemon, sliced

tonic water or sparkling
water

serves 4

Vodka and lime is a classic combination and here the drink is given a refreshing twist with the addition of a few drops of Angostura bitters.

Pour the vodka, lime cordial, and a little Angostura bitters into 4 tall glasses. Add ice cubes and lemon slices, top up with tonic water, and serve.

fruit and herb pimm's

1 bottle Pimm's No 1

2 cups strawberries, hulled
and cut in half

½ melon, seeded and
chopped, or nectarine slices

1 unwaxed lemon, sliced

½ cucumber, sliced

a few fresh mint leaves

a few fresh borage flowers
(optional)

to serve

ice cubes

1 bottle lemonade or
ginger ale, about 1 quart

serves 12

A balmy summer's evening seems the perfect time for a glass of Pimm's. This bittersweet liqueur-like drink, flavored with herbs and spices, was invented in the 1880s. Combine it with fresh fruit and mint for a perfect summer cooler.

Pour the Pimm's into a large pitcher and add the halved strawberries, melon or nectarine slices, lemon slices, cucumber slices, and some mint and borage flowers, if using. Set aside to steep for 30 minutes. Pour into tall glasses filled with ice cubes and top up with lemonade or ginger ale.

This tastes and looks heavenly, but has the effect of dynamite! If you can't get seedless watermelon, just use a regular one and seed it.

vodka watermelon

1 seedless watermelon, chilled

1 bottle chilled vodka, 750 ml

to serve

lime wedges

ice cubes

serves 20

Cut the melon in half and scoop out all the flesh. Put it in a blender and process until smooth. Remove to a large pitcher, add the vodka, and let chill for 2 hours before serving. Serve with lime wedges and ice.

variation Replace the vodka with sparkling water, or lemonade for those with a sweet tooth.

lemon soda
with mint and bitters

1 quart lemon soda or lemonade

6 sprigs of mint

Angostura bitters

lemon slices

ice cubes

serves 6

A delightfully simple drink, ideal for hot summer days. The bitters give the lemon soda a refreshing, herbal flavor and make it a pretty pale pink.

Pour the lemon soda or lemonade into 6 tall glasses. Add a sprig of mint, a few drops of bitters, slices of lemon, and ice cubes to each one, then serve at once.

stick drinks

You can use almost any fruit in a stick drink, as long as you include chopped limes and sugar.

lime and mint stick drink

12 large fresh mint leaves
2 teaspoons brown sugar
1 lime, finely diced, including zest
ice cubes
2 large shots Bacardi rum
club soda

cocktail shaker or pitcher
2 cocktail glasses

serves 2

Put the mint leaves, sugar, and lime in a shaker or pitcher and mash with a stick or spoon until quite pulpy. Alternatively, use a mortar and pestle.

Fill 2 glasses with ice to chill them thoroughly, then tip the ice into the mashed mint mixture. Add the Bacardi to the mixture, shake well, then pour back into the glasses. Add a little club soda and serve.

kiwi fruit, passionfruit, and lime sticky

1 large lime, diced
1 large kiwi fruit, peeled and diced
12 fresh mint leaves
1 tablespoon sugar
1 large passionfruit, cut in half
ice cubes
2 large shots vodka

cocktail shaker or pitcher
2 cocktail glasses

serves 2

Put the lime and kiwi fruit in a shaker or pitcher, add the mint, sugar, and passionfruit pulp and seeds. Mash well until pulpy.

Fill 2 glasses with ice to chill them thoroughly, then tip the ice into the kiwi fruit mixture. Add the vodka, shake or stir well, then pour back into the glasses. Serve at once.

basics

Vinaigrette can be a simple thing—just oil, vinegar, or other acidulator such as citrus juice, plus salt and freshly ground black pepper. You can add lots of other things to ring the changes, see the variations given below. Use the best oil you can find, and use as little vinegar as possible.

vinaigrette

6 tablespoons extra virgin olive oil

1 tablespoon white wine vinegar

sea salt and freshly ground black pepper

makes about ½ cup

Put the oil, vinegar, salt, and pepper in a salad bowl and beat with a fork or small whisk.

variations Add 1 teaspoon Dijon mustard and beat well. The mustard helps form an emulsion.

Add 1 teaspoon harissa paste and beat well.

Use Japanese rice vinegar, which gives a mild, smooth taste, instead of white wine vinegar. You can also substitute red wine vinegar, sherry vinegar, cider vinegar, or others.

Use freshly squeezed lime or lemon juice instead of the vinegar.

Instead of extra virgin, use 2 tablespoons mild virgin olive oil and 3 tablespoons nut oil such as walnut, macadamia, or hazelnut. Nut oils turn rancid very quickly, so buy small quantities, keep them in the refrigerator and use quickly.

Heat the vinaigrette in a small saucepan over gentle heat until just warm, then pour over the salad.

pesto

Although in Italy pesto is only used with pasta, the rest of us have fallen in love with it. It makes a delicious addition to salad—potato, tomato, chickpeas, and beans—stirred through rice or couscous with extra herbs.

basil pesto

¼ cup pine nuts
4 garlic cloves, crushed
1 teaspoon sea salt
a large double handful of fresh basil leaves
⅓ cup freshly grated Parmesan cheese
½ cup extra virgin olive oil, or to taste

makes about 1 cup

Put the pine nuts in a dry skillet and sauté gently and quickly until golden (about 30 seconds). They burn very easily, so don't leave them. Let cool. Transfer to a food processor or blender, add the garlic, salt, and basil, and blend to a paste. Add the Parmesan, blend again, then add the oil and blend again until smooth. Add extra oil if you want a looser texture.

red pesto

Instead of basil, use 8 oz. semi-dried tomatoes (or sun-dried tomatoes bottled in olive oil, but drained). A teaspoon of harissa paste lifts the flavor even further.

parsley pesto

Make basil pesto in full summer, when the leaves are big and full of their sweet, strong flavor. At other times, make a milder pesto using parsley, preferably the Italian flat-leaf variety.

arugula pesto

Use half parsley and half arugula leaves instead of the basil.

*2½ cups shredded
white cabbage*

1⅔ cups grated carrots

*½ white onion,
thinly sliced*

2 teaspoons sugar

*1 tablespoon white
wine vinegar*

*¼ cup Mayonnaise
(below)*

*2 tablespoons
heavy cream*

*1 tablespoon
whole-grain mustard*

*sea salt and freshly
ground black pepper*

serves 4

Homemade coleslaw is a million miles away from
the store-bought version. It's well worth the effort.

creamy coleslaw

Put the cabbage, carrots, and onion in a colander and
sprinkle with the 1 teaspoon salt, the sugar, and vinegar.
Stir well and let drain over a bowl for 30 minutes.

Squeeze out excess liquid from the vegetables and put
them in a large bowl. Put the mayonnaise, cream, and
mustard in a separate bowl and mix well, then stir into the
cabbage mixture. Season to taste with salt and pepper
and serve. Store in the refrigerator for up to 3 days.

mayonnaise

Don't use an extra virgin olive oil, otherwise
the sauce can become slightly bitter.

2 egg yolks

*2 teaspoons white wine
vinegar or freshly
squeezed lemon juice*

*2 teaspoons Dijon
mustard*

1¼ cups olive oil

*sea salt and freshly
ground black pepper*

makes about 1¼ cups

Put the egg yolks, vinegar, mustard, and ¼ teaspoon salt
in a food processor and blend briefly until frothy. With the
machine running, gradually pour in the olive oil in a slow,
steady stream, until all the oil is incorporated and the
sauce is thick and glossy.

If the sauce is too thick, add 1 to 2 tablespoons boiling
water and blend again briefly. Season to taste with salt
and pepper, then cover the surface of the mayonnaise
with plastic wrap. Store in the refrigerator for up to 3 days.

sauces

barbecue sauce

1 cup crushed tomatoes
½ cup maple syrup
2 tablespoons light molasses
2 tablespoons tomato ketchup
2 tablespoons white wine vinegar
3 tablespoons Worcestershire sauce
1 tablespoon Dijon mustard
1 teaspoon garlic powder
¼ teaspoon hot paprika
*sea salt and freshly ground
black pepper*

makes about 2 cups

Mix all the ingredients in a small saucepan, bring to a boil, and simmer gently for 10 to 15 minutes until reduced slightly and thickened. Season to taste with salt and pepper and let cool.

Pour into an airtight container and store in the refrigerator for up to 2 weeks.

asian barbecue sauce

½ cup crushed tomatoes
2 tablespoons hoisin sauce
1 teaspoon hot chile sauce
2 garlic cloves, crushed
2 tablespoons sweet soy sauce
1 tablespoon rice wine vinegar
1 teaspoon ground coriander
½ teaspoon ground cinnamon
¼ teaspoon Chinese five-spice powder

makes about 1½ cups

Mix all the ingredients in a small saucepan, add ½ cup water, bring to a boil, and simmer gently for 10 minutes. Remove from the heat and let cool.

Pour into an airtight container and store in the refrigerator for up to 2 weeks.

note The recipe for Reduced Balsamic Vinegar (far right) is given on page 147.

sweet chile sauce

*6 hot fresh red chiles, about 2 inches
long, seeded and chopped*
4 garlic cloves, chopped
1 teaspoon grated fresh ginger
1 teaspoon sea salt
½ cup rice wine vinegar
½ cup sugar

makes about 1 cup

Put the chiles, garlic, ginger, and salt in a food processor and blend to a coarse paste. Transfer to a saucepan, add the vinegar and sugar, bring to a boil, and simmer gently, partially covered, for 5 minutes until the mixture becomes a thin syrup. Remove from the heat and let cool.

Pour into an airtight container and store in the refrigerator for up to 2 weeks.

marinades

thai spice

2 stalks of lemongrass

6 kaffir lime leaves

2 garlic cloves, coarsely chopped

1 inch fresh ginger, coarsely chopped

4 cilantro roots or a handful of stems, washed and dried

2 small fresh red bird's eye chiles, seeded and coarsely chopped

1 cup extra virgin olive oil

2 tablespoons sesame oil

2 tablespoons Thai fish sauce

makes about 1½ cups

Using a sharp knife, trim the lemongrass stalk to 6 inches, then remove and discard the tough outer leaves. Chop the inner stalk coarsely.

Put the lemongrass, lime leaves, garlic, ginger, cilantro, and chiles in a mortar and pound with a pestle to release the aromas.

Put the mixture in a bowl, add the oils and fish sauce, and set aside to steep until ready to use.

minted yogurt

2 teaspoons coriander seeds

1 teaspoon cumin seeds

1 cup yogurt

2 tablespoons heavy cream

freshly squeezed juice of ½ lemon

1 tablespoon extra virgin olive oil

2 garlic cloves, crushed

1 teaspoon grated fresh ginger

½ teaspoon sea salt

2 tablespoons chopped fresh mint leaves

¼ teaspoon ground chiles

makes about 1¼ cups

Toast the coriander and cumin seeds in a dry skillet over medium heat until golden and aromatic, then let cool. Transfer to a spice grinder (or clean coffee grinder) and crush to a coarse powder.

Put the spices in a bowl, add the yogurt, cream, lemon juice, oil, garlic, ginger, salt, mint and ground chiles and mix well. Set aside to steep until ready to use.

herb, lemon, and garlic

2 sprigs of rosemary

2 sprigs of thyme

4 bay leaves

2 large garlic cloves, coarsely chopped

pared zest of 1 unwaxed lemon

1 teaspoon cracked black peppercorns

1 cup extra virgin olive oil

makes about 1¼ cups

Strip the rosemary and thyme leaves from the stalks and put them in a mortar. Add the bay leaves, garlic, and lemon zest, and pound with a pestle to release the aromas.

Put the mixture in a bowl and add the peppercorns and olive oil. Set aside to steep until ready to use.

index

A

aïoli, arugula 156

almond mascarpone cream, grilled figs with 188

anchovies: big Greek salad 43

Caesar salad 39

chicken Caesar wrap 76

delmonico steak with anchovy butter 172

marinated anchovies 24

pizza napoletana 130

salade niçoise 54

Spanish tart with peppers 133

summer vegetables with bagna cauda 16

antipasti, vegetable 140

Antipodean potato salad 52

Asian barbecue sauce 232

appetizers 9–33

arugula: arugula aïoli 156

arugula pesto 228

mozzarella, tomato, and arugula salad 36

asparagus: asparagus with prosciutto 23

salmon frittata with potatoes and asparagus 98

avocados: avocado salad 40

jerk chicken wings with avocado salsa 159

salt-crusted shrimp with tomato, avocado, and olive salad 147

B

bagna cauda, summer vegetables with 16

bananas: strawberry and banana ice cream shake 213

barbecue sauces 232

basil: basil oil 88, 118

basil pesto 228

beans: butterflied lamb with white bean salad 110

Italian bean dip 177

tonno e fagioli 56

beef: delmonico steak with anchovy butter 172

Thai-style beef salad 60

beet hummus with pan-grilled bread 180

blue and red berry tarts 195

bread: beet hummus with pan-grilled bread 180

Caesar salad 39

cherry tomato, bocconcini, and basil bruschetta 19

chicken panini with roasted pepper and arugula aïoli 156

chile spiked cornbread 168

focaccia with olives 183

grilled rosemary flatbread 184

pappa al pomodoro 15

souvlaki in pita 113

toasted ciabatta pizzas 68

Tuscan panzanella 47

bruschetta, cherry tomato, bocconcini, and basil 19

burgers, lamb 164

butterscotch sundae, hot 203

C

Caesar salad 39

cake, lemon with vanilla syrup and strawberries 196

Campari fizz 214

cannellini beans: tonno e fagioli 56

caramel: caramelized plum sherbet 199

nut brittle 203

champagne cocktails 214

cheese: big Greek salad 43

Caesar salad 39

cherry tomato, bocconcini, and basil bruschetta 19

Italian broiled bell pepper salad 44

mozzarella baked tomatoes 87

mozzarella, tomato, and arugula salad 36

pizza napoletana 130

radicchio with Gorgonzola and walnuts 20

slow-roasted tomatoes with ricotta and spaghetti 121

toasted ciabatta pizzas 68

Turkish pizza turnover 129

chicken: chicken and tarragon pesto pasta 75

chicken Caesar wrap 76

chicken lemon skewers 31

chicken panini with roasted pepper and arugula aïoli 156

chicken salad with radicchio and pine nuts 59

chicken skewers with thyme and sesame 160

Greek chicken stifado 105

jerk chicken with avocado salsa 159

paella 137

rosemary and lemon roasted chicken 106

chickpeas: hummus 179

lamb kabobs with warm chickpea salad 167

quick chickpea salad 48

chiles: grilled Mexican-style Cornish hens 163

chile spiked cornbread 168

chile tuna tartare pasta 125

grilled corn with chile-salt rub 83

smoky tomato salsa 171

sweet chile marinade 168

sweet chile sauce 232

chocolate: fudge sauce sundae 204

knickerbocker glory 200

s'mores 207

chorizo: chorizo in red wine 32

shrimp, chorizo, and sage skewers 94

clam packages with garlic butter 151

coconut milk: chilled coconut soup with sizzling shrimp 12

coconut ice cream 192

cod, broiled miso 102

coffee, iced 209

coleslaw, creamy 231

cordial, ginger and lime 210

corn: chile spiked cornbread 168

corn cakes 144

creamy corn salsa 163

grilled corn with chile-salt rub 83

Cornish hens, grilled Mexican-style 163

couscous salad, fragrant herb 51

cucumber: chilled coconut soup with sizzling shrimp 12

tzatziki 178

D

delmonico steak with anchovy butter 172

dips: hummus 179

Italian bean dip 177

tzatziki 178

dressings: Caesar 76

Dijon dressing 48

garlic dressing 113
lemon and cilantro dressing 97
lemon and herb 72
lime dressing 60
Marsala raisin dressing 59
vinaigrette 54, 227
drinks 208–23
duck, orange and soy glazed 109

E
eggplants with pesto sauce 84
eggs: mixed mushroom frittata 67
salmon frittata with potatoes and
asparagus 98

F
fava beans: Italian bean dip 177
figs, grilled with almond mascarpone
cream 188
fish: grilled fish bathed in oregano and
lemon 155
whole salmon stuffed with herbs 152
focaccia with olives 183
frittata: mixed mushroom 67
salmon with potatoes and asparagus 98
fruit: blue and red berry tarts 195
fruit frappé 208
grilled fruit packages 191
knickerbocker glory 200
fudge sauce sundae 204

G
garlic: arugula aïoli 156
clam packages with garlic butter 151
garlic dressing 113
herb, lemon, and garlic marinade 235
summer vegetables with bagna cauda 16
gazpacho 11
ginger and lime cordial 210
Greek chicken stifado 105
Greek salad 43
green beans: seared swordfish with new
potatoes, beans, and olives 101
grilling 139–73

H
haricot beans: butterflied lamb with white
bean salad 110

herb, lemon, and garlic marinade 235
hummus 179
beet hummus 180

I
ice cream: fudge sauce sundae 204
hot butterscotch sundae 203
knickerbocker glory 200
strawberry and banana ice cream
shake 213
toasted coconut ice cream 192
iced coffee 209
iced long vodka 218
Italian bean dip 177
Italian broiled bell pepper salad 44

J
jerk chicken wings with avocado salsa 159

K
kabobs: chicken lemon skewers 31
chicken skewers with thyme and
sesame 160
lamb kabobs with warm chickpea
salad 167
shrimp, chorizo, and sage skewers 94
kiwi fruit, passionfruit, and lime sticky 222
knickerbocker glory 200

L
lamb: butterflied lamb with white bean
salad 110
lamb burgers with mint yogurt 164
lamb kabobs with warm chickpea
salad 167
leeks: charred leeks with tarator sauce 143
lemon: herb, lemon, and garlic marinade 235
lemon cake with vanilla syrup and
strawberries 196
lemon soda with mint and bitters 221
lime: ginger and lime cordial 210
kiwi fruit, passionfruit and lime sticky 222
lime and mint stick drink 222
lime dressing 60

M
macadamia nuts: charred leeks with
tarator sauce 143
marinades 235

Marsala raisin dressing 59
marshmallows: s'mores 207
mascarpone: grilled figs with almond
mascarpone cream 188
mayonnaise 231
tiger shrimp with herb mayonnaise 79
Mexican-style Cornish hens 163
milk: iced coffee 209
vanilla milkshake 213
mint: lamb burgers with mint yogurt 164
lemon soda with mint and bitters 221
lime and mint stick drink 222
minted yogurt marinade 235
miso cod 102
mozzarella baked tomatoes 87
mozzarella, tomato, and arugula salad 36
mushroom frittata 67
mussels: seafood spaghettini 126
mustard: Dijon dressing 48

O
oil, basil 88, 118
olives: big Greek salad 43
focaccia with olives 183
Greek chicken stifado 105
marinated black olives 64
pizza napoletana 130
rosemary and lemon roasted chicken 106
salade niçoise 54
salt-crusted shrimp with tomato,
avocado, and olive salad 147
seared swordfish with new potatoes,
beans, and olives 101
simple tomato and olive tart 88
oranges: Mimosa 214

orange and soy glazed duck 109
strawberry, pear and orange frappé 210
orzo salad with lemon and herb dressing 72

P

paella 137
pancetta: avocado salad 40
pappa al pomodoro 15
pappardelle with basil oil 118
parsley pesto 228
passionfruit, kiwi fruit, and lime sticky 222
pasta: chicken and tarragon pesto pasta 75
    chile tuna tartare pasta 125
    orzo salad with lemon and herb
        dressing 72
    pappardelle with basil oil 118
    pasta with fresh tomato 117
    seafood spaghettini 126
    slow-roasted tomatoes with ricotta and
        spaghetti 121
    smoked salmon in lemon cream sauce
        with dill tagliatelle 122
pear, strawberry, and orange frappé 210
peas: fresh pea and lettuce risotto 134
    paella 137
peppers: chicken panini with roasted
        pepper and arugula aïoli 156
    Italian broiled bell pepper salad 44
    Spanish tart with peppers 133
pesto: arugula pesto 228
    baked eggplants with pesto sauce 84
    basil pesto 228
    chicken and tarragon pesto pasta 75
    parsley pesto 228

red pesto 228
picnics 63–79
Pimm's, fruit and herb 218
pineapple: fudge sauce sundae 204
    toasted coconut ice cream with grilled
        pineapple 192
pizzas: pizza napoletana 130
    toasted ciabatta pizzas 68
    Turkish pizza turnover 129
plum sherbet, caramelized 199
pork: paella 137
    sage-rubbed pork chops 171
    souvlaki in pita 113
    Tex-Mex pork rack 168
potatoes: Antipodean potato salad 52
    salade niçoise 54
    salmon frittata with potatoes and
        asparagus 98
    seared swordfish with new potatoes,
        beans, and olives 101
prosciutto, asparagus with 23

Q

quiche, zucchini 91

R

radicchio: chicken salad with radicchio
        and pine nuts 59
    radicchio with Gorgonzola and walnuts 20
red pesto 228
rice: fresh pea and lettuce risotto 134
    paella 137
risotto, fresh pea and lettuce 134
rosemary: grilled rosemary flatbread 184
    rosemary and lemon roasted chicken 106

S

sage-rubbed pork chops 171
salads 35–61
    Antipodean potato salad 52
    avocado salad 40
    big Greek salad 43
    butterflied lamb with white bean salad 110
    Caesar salad 39
    chicken Caesar wrap 76
    chicken salad with radicchio and pine
        nuts 59
    fragrant herb couscous salad 51
    Italian broiled bell pepper salad 44

lamb kabobs with chickpea salad 167
mozzarella, tomato, and arugula salad 36
orzo salad with lemon and herb dressing 72
quick chickpea salad 48
salade niçoise 54
salt-crusted shrimp with tomato,
    avocado, and olive salad 147
souvlaki in pita 113
summer salad 71
Thai-style beef salad 60
Tuscan panzanella 47
salmon: salmon frittata with potatoes and
    asparagus 98
    smoked and fresh salmon terrine 27
    whole salmon stuffed with herbs 152
salsas: avocado salsa 159
    creamy corn salsa 163
    salsa verde 110
    smoky tomato salsa 171
salt-crusted shrimp 147
sauces: Asian barbecue sauce 232
    barbecue sauce 232
    sweet chile sauce 232
sausages: chorizo in red wine 32
    shrimp, chorizo, and sage skewers 94
scallops with lemongrass and lime butter 148
seafood spaghettini 126
shrimp: chilled coconut soup with sizzling
    shrimp 12
    paella 137
    salt-crusted shrimp with tomato,
        avocado, and olive salad 147
    shrimp, chorizo, and sage skewers 94
    tiger shrimp with herb mayonnaise 79
smoked salmon: smoked and fresh
    salmon terrine 27
    smoked salmon in lemon cream sauce
        with dill tagliatelle 122
s'mores 207
snapper: grilled fish bathed in oregano
    and lemon 155
sherbet, caramelized plum 199
soups: chilled coconut soup with sizzling
    shrimp 12
    gazpacho 11
    pappa al pomodoro 15
souvlaki in pita 113
spaghetti: pasta with fresh tomato 117

slow-roasted tomatoes with ricotta
    and spaghetti 121
spaghettini, seafood 126
Spanish tart with peppers 133
squid: fried squid Roman-style 28
    seared squid with lemon and
        cilantro dressing 97
stews: Greek chicken stifado 105
stick drinks 222
strawberries: fruit and herb Pimm's 218
    fudge sauce sundae 204
    lemon cake with vanilla syrup and
        strawberries 196
    strawberry and banana ice cream
        shake 213
    strawberry, pear, and orange
        frappé 210
summer salad 71
summer vegetables with bagna
    cauda 16
sundaes: fudge sauce sundae 204
    hot butterscotch sundae 203
swordfish, seared with new potatoes,
    beans, and olives 101

T
tagliatelle: smoked salmon in lemon
    cream sauce with dill tagliatelle 122
tamarillos: Antipodean potato salad 52
tarator sauce, charred leeks with 143
tarts: blue and red berry tarts 195
    simple tomato and olive tart 88
    Spanish tart with peppers 133
terrine, smoked and fresh salmon 27
Tex-Mex pork rack 168
Thai spice marinade 235
Thai-style beef salad 60
tiger shrimp with herb mayonnaise 79
tomatoes: barbecue sauce 232
    cherry tomato, bocconcini, and
        basil bruschetta 19
    gazpacho 11
    Greek chicken stifado 105
    mozzarella baked tomatoes 87
    mozzarella, tomato, and arugula
        salad 36
    paella 137
    pappa al pomodoro 15
    pasta with fresh tomato 117

pizza napoletana 130
red pesto 228
salt-crusted shrimp with tomato,
    avocado, and olive salad 147
simple tomato and olive tart 88
slow-roasted tomatoes with ricotta
    and spaghetti 121
smoky tomato salsa 171
toasted ciabatta pizzas 68
Tuscan panzanella 47
tonno e fagioli 56
tuna: chile tuna tartare pasta 125
    salade niçoise 54
    tonno e fagioli 56
Turkish pizza turnover 129
Tuscan panzanella 47
tzatziki 178

V
vanilla milkshake 213
vegetables: summer vegetables with
    bagna cauda 16
    vegetable antipasti 140
vegetarian dishes 81–91
vinaigrette 54, 227
vodka: iced long vodka 218
    vodka watermelon 221

W
walnuts, radicchio with Gorgonzola
    and 20
watercress: summer salad 71
watermelon, vodka 221
wine: champagne cocktails 214
    chorizo in red wine 32
    Marsala raisin dressing 59
    white wine spritzer 217
wrap, chicken Caesar 76

Y
yogurt: chicken lemon skewers 31
    garlic dressing 113
    grilled fruit packages 191
    lamb burgers with mint yogurt 164
    minted yogurt marinade 235
    tzatziki 178

Z
zahtar spice mix 160
zucchini quiche 91

conversion charts

Weights and measures have been rounded
up or down slightly to make measuring easier.

Volume equivalents:

American	Metric	Imperial
1 teaspoon	5 ml	
1 tablespoon	15 ml	
¼ cup	60 ml	2 fl.oz.
⅓ cup	75 ml	2½ fl.oz.
½ cup	125 ml	4 fl.oz.
⅔ cup	150 ml	5 fl.oz. (¼ pint)
¾ cup	175 ml	6 fl.oz.
1 cup	250 ml	8 fl.oz.

Weight equivalents: Measurements:

Imperial	Metric	Inches	Cm
1 oz.	25 g	¼ inch	5 mm
2 oz.	50 g	½ inch	1 cm
3 oz.	75 g	¾ inch	1.5 cm
4 oz.	125 g	1 inch	2.5 cm
5 oz.	150 g	2 inches	5 cm
6 oz.	175 g	3 inches	7 cm
7 oz.	200 g	4 inches	10 cm
8 oz. (½ lb.)	250 g	5 inches	12 cm
9 oz.	275 g	6 inches	15 cm
10 oz.	300 g	7 inches	18 cm
11 oz.	325 g	8 inches	20 cm
12 oz.	375 g	9 inches	23 cm
13 oz.	400 g	10 inches	25 cm
14 oz.	425 g	11 inches	28 cm
15 oz.	475 g	12 inches	30 cm
16 oz. (1 lb.)	500 g		
2 lb.	1 kg		

Oven temperatures:

110°C	(225°F)	Gas ¼
120°C	(250°F)	Gas ½
140°C	(275°F)	Gas 1
150°C	(300°F)	Gas 2
160°C	(325°F)	Gas 3
180°C	(350°F)	Gas 4
190°C	(375°F)	Gas 5
200°C	(400°F)	Gas 6
220°C	(425°F)	Gas 7
230°C	(450°F)	Gas 8
240°C	(475°F)	Gas 9

credits

Photographs

Ian Wallace Back endpapers right, pages 3 background, inset left & inset center right, 6 right, 6–7, 9 inset center left & right, 13, 14, 17, 34, 35 inset left & inset center right, 58, 61, 63 inset center right, 66, 73, 77, 78, 81 inset center left, 82, 92, 93 background, insets left & center right, 95, 103, 108, 111, 115 inset center left, 120, 128, 135, 136 insets left, center left & right, 141–150, 153, 154, 157, 161–173, 175 insets left & center left, 181, 185, 187 background, inset center left & center right, 189, 190, 193, 198, 199, 206, 211, 212, 215, 219, 221, 223, 225 insets right & center left, 230, 233, 234

Debi Treloar Pages 1, 2, 3 inset center left & inset right, 4, 5, 63 background & inset left, 69, 70, 74, 81 inset center right, 85, 86, 107, 139 inset center right, 158, 174, 175 background, 186, 187 inset left, 194, 201–205, 208, 209, 216, 220

Peter Cassidy Pages 10, 16, 21, 25, 29, 30, 33, 35 inset right, 37–57, 65, 81 inset left, 89, 90, 96, 100, 116, 124, 178, 179, 182, 225 insets left & center right, 226, 229, 238

Martin Brigdale Pages 22, 93 insets right & center left, 104, 112, 115 insets left, center right & right, 119, 131, 132, 136, 175 inset center right, 176

William Lingwood Pages 26, 31, 67, 99, 101, 106, 123, 126–127, 133, 151, 180, 228

Jan Baldwin Pages 8, 9 inset left & center right, 35 background & inset center left, 115 background, 225 background

Christopher Drake Back endpapers left, pages 62, 63 insets right & center right, 138, 187 inset right

Pia Tryde Front endpapers right, pages 81 background & inset right, 114

Nicky Dowey Pages 23, 36, 60, 237

Chris Tubbs Front endpapers left, pages 9 background, 80, 240

Gus Filgate Pages 18, 175 inset right

David Brittain Pages 6 left, 224

Caroline Arber Page 87

Polly Wreford Page 139 background

Francesca Yorke Page 214

Recipes

LOUISE PICKFORD

Beet hummus with pan-grilled bread
Broiled miso cod
Butterflied lamb with white bean salad
Caramelized plum sherbet
Champagne cocktails
Charred leeks with tarator sauce
Chicken caesar wraps
Chicken lemon skewers
Chicken panini with roasted pepper and arugula aïoli
Chicken salad with radicchio and pine nuts
Chicken skewers with lemon and thyme
Chilled coconut soup with sizzling shrimp
Chile tuna tartare pasta
Clam packages with garlic butter
Coleslaw
Corn cakes
Delmonico steaks with anchovy butter
Fragrant herb couscous salad
Fresh pea and lettuce risotto
Fruit and herb Pimm's
Ginger and lime cordial
Grilled corn with chile-salt rub
Grilled figs with almond mascarpone cream
Grilled fish bathed in oregano and lemon
Grilled fruit packages
Grilled Mexican-style Cornish hens
Grilled rosemary flatbread
Iced long vodka
Jerk chicken wings with avocado salsa
Lamb burgers with mint yogurt
Lamb kabobs with warm chickpea salad
Lemon soda with mint and bitters
Lemon cake with vanilla syrup and strawberries
Marinades
Mayonnaise
Mixed mushroom frittata
Orange and soy glazed duck
Orzo salad with lemon and herb dressing
Pappa al pomodoro
Pasta with fresh tomato
Sage-rubbed pork chops
Salt-crusted shrimp with tomato, avocado, and olive salad
Sauces
Scallops with lemongrass and lime butter
Seared squid with lemon and cilantro dressing
Seared swordfish with new potatoes, beans, and olives
Shrimp, chorizo, and sage skewers
Simple tomato and olive tart
Slow-roasted tomatoes with ricotta and spaghetti
S'Mores
Stick drinks
Strawberry and banana ice cream shake
Strawberry, pear, and orange frappé
Summer vegetables with bagna cauda
Tex-mex pork rack
Thai-style beef salad
Tiger shrimp with herb mayonnaise
Toasted coconut ice cream with grilled pineapple
Turkish pizza turnover
Vegetable antipasti
Whole salmon stuffed with herbs

ELSA PETERSEN-SCHEPELERN

Avocado salad
Caesar salad
Fruit frappé
Fudge sauce sundae
Greek salad
Hot butterscotch sundae
Iced coffee
Italian broiled bell pepper salad
Knickerbocker glory
Pesto
Quick chickpea salad
Salade Niçoise
Tonno e fagioli
Tuscan panzanella
Vanilla milkshake
Vinaigrette

CLARE FERGUSON

Antipodean potato salad
Asparagus with prosciutto
Focaccia with olives
Greek chicken stifado
Hummus
Italian bean dip
Marinated black olives
Mozzarella, tomato, and arugula salad
Paella
Pappardelle with basil oil
Pizza napoletana
Radicchio with gorgonzola and walnuts
Souvlaki in pita
Spanish tart with peppers
Tzatziki

FRAN WARDE

Baked eggplants with pesto sauce
Blue and red berry tarts
Chicken and tarragon pesto pasta
Mozzarella baked tomatoes
Rosemary and lemon roasted chicken
Summer salad
Toasted ciabatta pizzas
Vodka watermelon
White wine spritzer

JULZ BERESFORD

Chorizo in red wine
Fried squid Roman-style
Gazpacho
Marinated anchovies

MAXINE CLARK

Cherry tomato, bocconcini, and basil bruschetta
Salmon frittata with potatoes and asparagus
Salmon in lemon cream sauce with dill tagliatelle
Smoked and fresh salmon terrine

SILVANA FRANCO

Seafood spaghettini

LESLEY WATERS

Zucchini quiche with sun-dried tomatoes